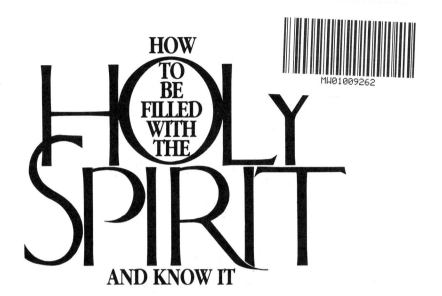

HOW TO BE FILLED WITH THE HOLY SPIRIT AND KNOW IT

HOW TO BE FILLED WITH THE HOLY SPIRIT AND KNOW IT

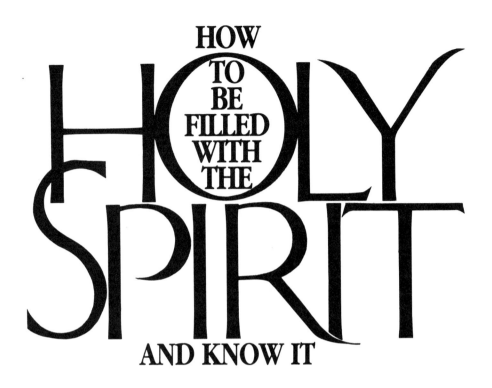

GARRIE F. WILLIAMS

REVIEW AND HERALD® PUBLISHING ASSOCIATION
HAGERSTOWN, MD 21740

Copyright © 1991 by
Review and Herald® Publishing Association

The author assumes full responsibility for the accuracy of all facts and quotations as cited in this book.

This book was
Edited by James Cavil
Designed by Bill Kirstein
Cover art by Helcio Deslandes
Typeset: 11/12 Garamond Book

PRINTED IN U.S.A.

96 95 94 93 92   10 9 8 7 6 5 4

R&H Cataloging Service
Williams, Garrie F.
    How to be filled with the Holy
Spirit and know it.

    1. Holy Spirit. 2. Gifts, Spiritual.
I. Title.
        231.3

ISBN 0-8280-0633-4

To Barbara

whose total dedication as
a wife and mother
has illustrated for me many times
God's steadfast love.

Acknowledgments

This book has been made possible only by the direct leading and constant help of the Holy Spirit. All praise will go to Him, although I take full responsibility for any lack of skill displayed. I could not begin to thank all those whom the Holy Spirit has used to inspire and advise me in the writing of this book. The pastors who have shared in Holy Spirit Fellowships have been a great source of strength. Kevin Wilfley has prayed with me many times and has provided invaluable research and study. I thank him for permission to use his list of Bible references to the Holy Spirit. Don and Ruthie Jacobsen have taught me much about prayer and the Holy Spirit and have provided me with the opportunities that made possible much of the study and experiences that form the foundation of this work. My secretary, Carolyn Rawson, has aided me greatly in bringing each chapter of the manuscript into its final form. The pressure of this along with the heavy load of our routine work she has carried with a spirit of Christian dedication and cheerfulness. Especially I want to thank my wife, Barbara, who has lived through many of the events recorded in this book and whose continued prayers, support, and encouragement have enabled me to do much more for the Lord than I could ever have done alone. All of the experiences and stories I have used in this book are true, although some names have been changed.

Contents

Orientation

Some time ago a well-known author introduced his latest book with the question "Why another book on spiritual gifts?" I ask a similar question. Why another book on the Holy Spirit? Much excellent material has been written on this topic, and yet I have noticed a thirst for more.

The German university professor and Lutheran theologian Helmut Thielicke quoted from British Baptist Charles Spurgeon, who began a chapter on the Holy Spirit by saying, "I have selected a topic upon which it would be difficult to say anything which has not been often said before: but as the theme is of the highest importance, it is good to dwell upon it frequently, and even if we bring forth only old things and nothing more, it may be wise to put you in remembrance of them." Over the past year I have read 30 or 40 books about the Holy Spirit, as well as surveying at least 300 more. Some have been deep theological theses with words that sent me searching dictionaries in a half dozen languages. Others have been deeply devotional, bringing me to my knees to open my heart before God for the blessings of the Spirit. A few have been argumentative, with a special ax to grind. These sometimes left me feeling perplexed and even discouraged.

While attempting to steer a course through these various approaches to the subject I have not tried to compete with the depth and breadth of classic works on this topic by such recognized authorities as R. A. Torrey, Andrew Murray, and L. E. Froom, to name a few.

During my discussions of the Holy Spirit throughout the past year with groups of church leaders, pastors, and lay members in eight or nine countries a number of specific needs and questions have arisen, such as: "Why don't we have study guides on this topic?" "Are there some recent evidences of the working of the Holy Spirit?" "Why don't we really know the Holy Spirit as a person rather than a theory or a topic?" "How can we avoid the extremes of emotionalism and cold negativism?" "What is the certain evidence that a person has been filled with the Holy Spirit?"

On top of these and many similar questions I detect an earnest desire for more understanding of the Holy Spirit in various and sometimes surprising places. While I was conducting a Holy Spirit Fellowship for pastors on a university campus a number of students expressed regret that the meetings were not for them. "This is what we need. We want to know more about the Holy Spirit," they said.

A senior citizen spoke recently to his church, "The reason for the problems we are seeing today in our own lives and the lives of many of our young people is that we older church members have neglected to understand and be filled with the Holy Spirit." More than 50 immediately signed up for a special study class.

Academy students who were considered the "cool" people among their peers surprised everyone by their enthusiasm for the Holy Spirit and their new fire for God. A dentist told me of all-night prayer meetings in his church and how church members of all ages are thirsting for the Holy Spirit and being filled daily.

"I have a group of physicians and students who are gathering with me each week to study and pray about the Holy Spirit," a medical school professor informed me. A deep earnestness and joy in his life testified to the reality of his own fellowship with the Holy Spirit.

In this book I have endeavored to meet some of these expressed needs by including study guides with each chapter and incorporating personal experiences of the working of the Holy Spirit along with some theological discussion.

I have written with neighborhood study groups foremost in mind, while at the same time realizing that many of these groups may actually meet in churches, on college and academy campuses, and various retreat and seminar situations.

The study guides use relational and inductive questions that are not primarily for teaching but rather discussion and interaction. Relational questions help us understand God, ourselves, other people, and the world around us. These questions do not major in presenting intellectual facts, but rather lead into an understanding of what is involved in strong and positive relationships in these four critical areas.

Inductive Bible study has been called discovery Bible study. This type of study has been used with small groups for hundreds of years. Basically, in inductive Bible study there are three questions asked of each part of Scripture: "What does the text say?" "What does the text mean?" and "How can I apply this text and live according to Scripture today?"

If you are studying these guides in a small group, it is important that the group leader understand a few basic principles of facilitating a group. The leader does not have to be concerned about being a teacher, and knowing answers to complex theological questions. Rather, the group leader guides the group in discovery, discussion, prayer, and sharing with one another, as well as encouraging group members in outreach and growth of the group. It is good if each group can have a leader, an assistant leader, and a host or hostess. In this way the group will function successfully and, as it grows, may even want to divide into two or more smaller groups. It is best if the group does not reach beyond 12 or 14 members, as this will limit the opportunity for discussion and interaction.

Small group leaders will find great encouragement if they can meet with other leaders on a regular basis. In this regular meeting they can receive, especially from their pastor, encouragement, help, and inspiration that they, in turn, can share with their own small group in the weekly Bible study.

My earnest prayer for you is that the Holy Spirit will not be just a topic of theological discussion or a theoretical sequence of facts to add to your inventory of biblical knowledge, but a friend—a person you will know and love. In daily fellowship with the Holy Spirit you can be a Christian of spiritual power and victory. Yes, I pray that in your life and mine through the ministry of the Holy Spirit Jesus will be glorified and His Word exalted. May our heavenly Father be worshiped. To Him we give honor and praise as we think of what He has done and will do through the mighty power of the Holy Spirit.

CHAPTER ONE

Love Casts Out Fear — of the Spirit

A ll my life I have believed that it is risky to pray for the Holy Spirit."
The church member who said this to me struggled to grasp the
reality of the boundless love of God. This love is revealed in the gift of the
Holy Spirit (Romans 5:5). Why would anyone fear the Holy Spirit? It is
like fearing love.

To fear the Holy Spirit is to fear a friend. The Holy Spirit is a person,
not a force like gravity or an energy like electricity. The Holy Spirit, as a
person, represents Jesus with all His unfailing love (John 16:13, 14).

While some churches seem to reveal an overfamiliarity with the Spirit,
others have a chronic pneumaphobia. They talk and sing about the Spirit
and even politely pray about Him, but real Spirit power is about as rare
as unpolluted air in Los Angeles.

Some Christians have been very cautious about the Holy Spirit. Even
though the Holy Spirit is mentioned more times than the Sabbath in the
New Testament (you can find more than 250 references), I cannot
remember in the first 15 years of my ministry preaching more than two
or three positive sermons on the Holy Spirit, even though I spoke many
times of the necessity of true worship and the dangers of some forms of
so-called Holy Spirit revival.

What are some of the fears of the Holy Spirit that have caused us to
treat Him like a distant cousin of leprosy?

Terrorized by Tongues

A misuse of the gift of tongues has been seen as an ever-present
danger. Some time ago a man gave me a demonstration of his glossolaliac
ability, holding forth in a series of sounds that he claimed was the
language of heaven. Although I have heard this version of tongues many
times over the past 25 years I am yet to be convinced that heaven sounds
like that.

The insistence of some denominations that tongues are the paramount sign of Spirit baptism and that non-tongue speakers are second-class Christians has added to the confusion. So has the diversity of tongues experiences among some Christian and non-Christian groups in many parts of the world. Unusual vocal sounds have been connected to highly intense religious practices for many thousands of years.

The question that remains, however, is "Is the baptism of the Holy Spirit to be neglected, ignored, or refused because of distortions or counterfeits of the gift of tongues?" "There are diversities of gifts, but the same Spirit" (1 Corinthians 12:4).

Embarrassed by Emotionalism

Some have feared emotionalism. For years I majored in a rather intellectual form of Christianity that emphasized a discussion and dissemination of truth that bypassed the heart. People who wept and shouted praises were looked upon as rather superficial. Human excitement has always been a threat in a church that has worn lukewarmness like a mummy wrapping. It is possible that the baptism of the Holy Spirit may bring even to a sophisticated heart an irresistible, irrepressible feeling of joy. While the artificiality of emotionalism will be avoided, Spirit-filled Christians are not embarrassed with the feelings of praise and rejoicing which engulf them. "For the kingdom of God is not food and drink, but righteousness and peace and joy in the Holy Spirit" (Romans 14:17).

Sidestepping Truth

I have noticed that some who profess to be filled with the Spirit seem to be the most resistant to truth. As an evangelist preaching the great doctrines of the Word, I was often dismayed to discover that subjective feelings masqueraded as Spirit-guidance in some religious circles. My array of proof texts had no effect in the face of this. Even though a "thus saith the Lord" clearly outlined a biblical standard for a born-again Christian life, people who professed to be filled with the Spirit would often say, "We will pray about this. We will see how the Lord leads us by His Spirit." Imagine being confronted with the commandment that says, "Thou shalt not commit adultery," and saying I will pray about this, I will seek the wisdom of the Spirit as to whether this is something that the Lord wants me to do. The Holy Spirit, however, draws us to the truth and makes it clear to our minds. The purpose of the Spirit is to lead us into all truth and to give us the strength to obey (1 John 16:13; 1 Peter 1:22).

Worry About Worship

Culturally, since the 1860s my denomination has endeavored to look sophisticated in its form of worship. A relatively unconventional message has made it seem important to at least look dignified on Sabbath morning. Thus there has arisen a fear that the baptism of the Holy Spirit may somehow throw the church into the camp of the undignified and uncouth.

Fear of this unpredictability in worship has led to the neglect of the gift that can bring joyous corporate communion between God and His people. It is interesting though that Paul, as he spoke of the spiritual gifts and ministries that would dramatically affect Christian worship, showed how groundless these fears are when the Spirit really is in control. "For God is not the author of confusion but of peace, as in all the churches of the saints" (1 Corinthians 14:33). "Let all things be done decently and in order" (verse 40).

Negated by Neglect

Probably the saddest reason for the neglect of the power of the Holy Spirit is that the church has learned to do without it. I was shocked to read a statement concerning this a few years ago because it described my own condition in the ministry for many years. "The reason why there is so little of the Spirit of God manifested is that ministers learn to do without it." [1]

For most of the seventies and eighties I was absorbed in ministry, but basically ran on my own steam. I prayed a lot for others but little for myself. I studied the Bible to speak to others and convince others but very rarely to feed my own soul. My teenage experience of Spirit-filling was submerged under a flood of theological and methodological information and expertise. There was a lot of apparent success, but limited heart spirituality.

Because of the strong doctrinal basis of my denomination, churches have learned to function without the Holy Spirit while relying on teachings, traditions, training, and institutional respectability. Is it remotely possible that we have made commandments of God of no effect by our traditions (Matthew 15:3, 6)? Traditions are not wrong in themselves necessarily, but when they cause us to feel comfortable while neglecting such commandments as "Be filled with the Spirit," they become positively dangerous.

Marooned on the Island of Materialism

The grip of materialism and assorted sins tends to hold many church members in wary distance of a real Spirit-filled life. Complete surrender to the Holy Spirit is devastating to sin. Sin is revealed in all its ugliness by the Spirit and can no longer euphemistically be described as heredity, entertainment, or pleasure. Contrary to materialism is the sense of sacrifice that the Spirit brings into the Christian life. Sacrifice, in fact, is sudden death to materialism with all its shallow joys. Notice what happened when the Spirit moved powerfully upon these early Christians. "And when they had prayed, the place where they were assembled together was shaken; and they were all filled with the Holy Spirit, and they spoke the word of God with boldness. Now the multitude of those who believed were of one heart and one soul; neither did anyone say that any of the things he possessed was his own, but they had all things in common. And with great power the apostles gave witness to the resurrection of the Lord Jesus. And great grace was upon them all. Nor was there anyone among them who lacked; for all who were possessors of lands or houses sold them, and brought their proceeds of the things that were sold, and laid them at the apostles' feet; and they distributed to each as anyone had need" (Acts 4:31-35).

Majoring in Minors

Strangely enough, in my own life and ministry it was not primarily fears that really held me back from total surrender to the Spirit of God, but rather the dominance of minor matters. I have taken seriously the following statement: "If all were willing, all would be filled with the Spirit. Wherever the need of the Holy Spirit is a matter little thought of, there is seen spiritual drought, spiritual darkness, spiritual declension and death. Whenever minor matters occupy the attention, the divine power which is necessary for the growth and prosperity of the church, and which would bring all other blessings in its train, is lacking, though offered in infinite plentitude." [2]

Minor matters are important, but when they dominate they are dangerous. The color of new paint for the church basement is a minor matter in the light of eternity, but an issue such as this has been known to consume numerous church board hours in a church that is too busy to pray. Even major matters such as family togetherness or a mighty evangelistic outreach must not replace reliance on the Holy Spirit, who will bring all other necessary blessings with Him.

Our newest son-in-law, Glen, joined the police force after leaving college, and eventually attended law school and became a prosecutor. During our first Christmas together he gripped our attention with stories of terrible murders he had investigated. Out walking one day down a deserted bush track in Sydney, I came across a body lying in a contorted position on the rocky ground. Thinking of all the recent stories that I had heard, I ran for help, supposing I had found a murder victim. When help arrived, we discovered that the man had lain there all night under the influence of alcohol. "He thought you were dead," one of the rescuers said, pointing the revived man to me. "I feel dead," he mumbled with a strange laugh. I did not feel like laughing at all, but was rather embarrassed. Many people have looked at the church and thought it dead, when in reality it has simply become intoxicated by success in relatively minor matters.

Since October 1986, when I made a commitment to spend an hour each day in prayer, I have noticed that minor matters have moved away from center stage in my life and that every barrier to the daily filling of the Spirit in my life has evaporated like water on a hot stove. I now know many others who are experiencing this joy. Love is poured into our hearts by the Holy Spirit, and that love banishes fear (1 John 4:18).

With the Word of God constantly before us to verify every experience and to safeguard us from our own imagination, we learn the inexpressible joy of fellowship with the Spirit of God (Philippians 2:1; 2 Corinthians 13:14). This certainty is sweeping the church today like a tidal wave—a great tsunami that will reach its peak in the latter rain of the Spirit.

Love Casts Out Fear—of the Spirit

Cohesive Contrasts

People meeting in small groups more than 200 years ago developed what have become known as the "Quaker questions." Use these now to get to know others in your group. The first two are answered briefly, with more time given to the second pair of questions.

1. Where were you living when you were age 9?

2. How did you heat your house at age 9?

3. When you were 9, who or what was your center of emotional warmth?

4. When did God become more than just a name to you?

Consideration of the Word
Study Text: Acts 2

How would you describe your present feelings regarding the Holy Spirit?

Fear _____ Suspicion _____ Ignorance _____

Unconcern _____ Excitement _____ Joy _____

Desire to learn _____ Other _____

What do you think is the reason for this feeling you have toward the Holy Spirit?

_____

Read Acts 2:1-13. What differing reactions became evident among the crowd who first saw the disciples filled with the Holy Spirit?_____

_____

Review the seven reasons for fear or disregard of the Holy Spirit that were
studied in chapter one. How many of these issues do you see surfacing in
Acts 2?_____

_____

Why are special new revelations of the Holy Spirit's power so difficult for many
to accept?_____

_____

_____

_____

Read Acts 2:37-47. Notice that some "gladly received" the words they heard
after having been "cut to the heart." Why is this shift of feeling easy for some and
hard for others?_____

_____

List some of the "minor matters" that seem most effective today in keeping
people from a deep and joyful relationship with God._____

_____

Apparently the Holy Spirit will help minor matters assume their rightful place in
our lives. If you feel concerned about allowing God to center your life upon
things of eternal value, compare now Romans 5:5 and 1 John 4:18. What
method do you see God using to evaporate those fears?_____

_____

If the kingdom of God were revealed today, what would be its dominant characteristics according to Romans 14:17? How do you feel about this?_____

Conversation With the Lord

Let each group member who feels comfortable interact in prayer with each other and the Lord.

First, pray brief prayers of praise.

Second, pray for the Holy Spirit to lead in love and fill each life.

Finally, pray for any specific needs group members have expressed.

Close the group meeting by praying the Lord's Prayer together.

Committing the Word to Memory

This week, write out Acts 2:38, 39. Memorize these verses, then share them with someone as soon as possible.

_____

_____

_____

_____

CHAPTER
TWO
▼

Amazing Grace Is a Person

Where is the Holy Spirit in relationship to an unconverted life? While this question may not have recently caused you sleepless nights, the same question asked another way may be particularly relevant. For instance, if your spouse or another family member has not given his or her life to Jesus and is wandering in a dangerous minefield of sin, you may ask, "What is God doing to answer my prayers for this person I love so much?"

According to Jesus, there is a definite difference between the Holy Spirit being *with* a person and being *in* a person (John 14:17). Paul writes in a way that is as clear as a mountain stream. "You are not in the flesh but in the Spirit, if indeed the Spirit of God dwells in you. Now if anyone does not have the Spirit of Christ, he is not His" (Romans 8:9). Apparently, either the Holy Spirit is present in a life, or that person is not a Christian. Or to put it the other way around, before a person is a born-again Christian, the Holy Spirit is not dwelling in the life.

Elective Extra or Essential?

When I went to buy a new car a few years ago, the salesman spent some time trying to convince me that I needed air conditioning and an automatic transmission. They were optional extras. But at no time did the salesman inquire as to whether or not I wanted an engine in the car. The engine is not an optional extra but an essential. If the Holy Spirit is much more essential to the Christian life than an engine is to a car, how does an unbeliever come to the place where the Holy Spirit takes up residence in his or her life? Another question as equally important: "How can 'engineless,' or powerless, unbelievers move ahead to the place where they can accept Jesus as their Saviour?" Nothing will help more in answering these questions than understanding the external workings of the Holy Spirit as He surrounds each unconverted life with the grace of God.

As a child I never once attended a Sunday school or Sabbath school. Once each week, though, there was a time of religious instruction in my public school. For some reason I usually sat at the back of the class and constantly caused a disturbance. I did, however, learn the song "Jesus Loves Me" in two languages. In my early teen years I opened my heart to Jesus and asked Him to come into my life.

Did the Holy Spirit have anything to do with me before I was converted? Paul says to Titus, "For the grace of God that brings salvation has appeared to all men, teaching us that, denying ungodliness and worldly lusts, we should live soberly, righteously, and godly in the present age" (Titus 2:11, 12). Paul seems to indicate here that the grace of God works upon the heart of every person who has entered this world, helping each one to understand that there is a better way of life, that there is not only forgiveness for sin, but strength for victory. Of course, Paul goes on to explain that salvation actually comes through the kindness, love, and mercy of God and that the fruitage of a better way of life is a result of salvation and the power of the Holy Spirit.

Now, that is a lot for an unconverted person to swallow, but in the simplest terms it is an explanation of total forgiveness and daily victory by the grace of God. The Holy Spirit working in a life before conversion is what John Wesley calls prevenient grace. That is, grace available previous to conversion.

Coming to Grips With Grace

Only fairly recently did I find a new revelation of God's truth when I discovered that very often grace in the New Testament refers to the power of the Holy Spirit. It says that when the Holy Spirit filled the disciples, "great grace was upon them all" (Acts 4:33). Because of the power of grace, it is possible to do many good works (2 Corinthians 9:8). In fact, Paul was clearly told by God, "My grace is sufficient for you, for My strength is made perfect in weakness" (2 Corinthians 12:9). It was through this grace that the power of God rested upon Paul and he clearly understood and taught that the power of God is actually the presence and working of the Holy Spirit (Ephesians 3:16, 20). At least twice it appears that the Holy Spirit is called the Spirit of grace (Zechariah 12:10; Hebrews 10:29).

Many times the definition of grace is given as simply the unmerited favor of God. That puzzled me, for while I knew that all we sinners receive from God is certainly unmerited and most assuredly salvation is totally unmerited, yet it clearly states that the grace of God was upon Jesus (Luke 2:40), and that we, as Christians, are to grow in grace (2 Peter 3:18). On top of this I discovered that many of the more than 700 references to grace in the writings of Ellen White, a Spirit-filled pioneer of my denomination, speak of it, not just as a benevolent, merciful attitude of God toward man, but directly as a power that works within a human life. For instance: "The only power that can create or perpetuate true peace is the grace of Christ." [1] John Wesley in his famous sermon 9 emphasized his strong conviction that grace and the Holy Spirit are synonymous.

Now, with this understanding of grace in mind I can look back on my own spiritual development, realizing that it was the power of the Spirit of grace that was leading me as a young person to Jesus. Eventually my mother was converted and began to search for a Bible-based church. I went with her as she visited many denominations, some centering on small groups in homes and others in ecclesiastical buildings of various vintages. The grace of God that brings salvation was appearing to me even as I remained unconverted. The breakup of my parents' marriage in an age and place where divorce was rare brought me heartache and self-blame, yet again produced an environment in which the Spirit could speak to my heart.

In the life of an unconverted person the Holy Spirit is at work constantly providing opportunities to desire a better way of life, sincerely come to repentance, and finally, invite Jesus into the heart (Genesis 6:3; John 16:13, 14). If this working of the Spirit is complemented by the intercessory prayers of Christians, the possibility of positive results are greatly multiplied. If Christians, at the right time and place, offer literature or personal testimony the power of grace can reach an unconverted yet surrendered heart and create the miracle of a life made new in Jesus Christ.

"Today this Spirit is constantly at work, seeking to draw the attention of men to the great sacrifice made upon the cross of Calvary, to unfold to the world the love of God to man, and to open to the unconverted soul the promises of the Scripture." [2]

The nineteenth-century equivalent of a commercial airline crash was shipwreck. Before an age of travel insurance, people set out for distant shores not knowing if they would reach their destination. Many nineteenth-century hymns used nautical terminology such as seamen, anchors, and storms because the uncertainty of ocean travel seemed to picture the dangers of life in general.

A heroine of the age of shipwreck was Grace Darling, the daughter of the lighthouse keeper at Longstone in the Farne Islands of the northeastern coast of England. Looking through the lighthouse telescope on the morning of September 7, 1838, Grace saw nine survivors of a terrible shipwreck clinging to a rock in the midst of the raging sea. Unable to find local men willing to row out in the rescue boat, Grace made two hazardous trips, first with her father and then with two of the men she had rescued. In the raging danger of the storm with wicked, ragged rocks threatening to rip the boat apart, Grace Darling was able to bring all nine survivors to safety.

"The grace of God that brings salvation has appeared to all men" (Titus 2:11). The Grace Darling of the Holy Spirit constantly comes alongside each unconverted life, offering the hope of love, peace, and joy in Jesus.

If you have accepted Jesus as your Saviour, take a few minutes to review the steps that led you to conversion. You will be able to list many evidences of the Spirit of prevenient grace leading you to salvation.

Recently I heard a good friend of mine talking about the marvelous grace of God that had led him to Jesus. In academy he was a student leader, but was popular because of a remarkable ability to tell dirty stories and use bad language. Whenever possible he squandered much of his valuable time watching television, and was expelled from class many times. "Throughout all of this," he said, "I remembered seeing my mother weeping as she read the beautiful story of Jesus in *The Desire of Ages*. That memory of a praying mother coincided with the message of an academy Week of Prayer speaker, and Larry gave his life to Jesus.

"I still remember shaking my fist at God. The last dream I had for my future was to be a pastor." But the Spirit of grace made possible the answers to a mother's prayer. "I was placed in a class with poor students," Larry said as he thought again of the pain of having to attend remedial homework sessions. "They told me I would never make it through college."

Eventually after his conversion he became student body president, and today Dr. Larry Evans is a minister and respected leader in the church. As with Saul, the Spirit of the Lord came upon this young person, and he was turned into another man (1 Samuel 10:6).

"Some seem to feel that they must be on probation, and must prove to the Lord that they have reformed, before they can claim His blessing. But they may claim the blessing of God even now. They must have His grace, the Spirit of Christ, to help their infirmities, or they cannot resist evil. Jesus loves to have us come to Him just as we are, sinful, helpless, dependent. We may come with all our weakness, our folly, our sinfulness, and fall at His feet in penitence. It is His glory to encircle us in the arms of His love and to bind up our wounds, to cleanse us from all impurity." [3]

Soliciting Spirit-Life

If you have not consciously accepted Jesus into your life, perhaps the Spirit of grace is convicting you that this is the time. I have prayed with many people who have taken this step, and I can assure you that it is the most important and wonderful experience in any life. The Spirit of grace and supplication will lead you to recognize your sins and you will mourn that Jesus had to suffer for you (Zechariah 12:10). Just tell Jesus that you are deeply sorry for what has happened and that you now accept Him into your life as Lord and King. Praise Him that He has saved you and that you are now part of His family in a special way. "For by grace you have been saved through faith, and that not of yourselves; it is the gift of God" (Ephesians 2:8).

I have found that many people who are culturally Christians have never taken the personal, conscious step of accepting Jesus as their Saviour. It is like belonging to a bicycle club, knowing all about bicycles, and yet never having had the experience of riding down a beautiful country lane with the scent of spring flowers in the air and the wind blowing through your hair.

One day our youngest daughter, Sharon, and I rode our bicycles through the lovely residential area near our home in Spokane. The uphill ride was rather tough, but soon we were out in the countryside, with trees and fields in all directions and snowcapped mountains in the distance. Toward home it was downhill most of the way, and the miles seemed to speed by. We felt good! All the theory in the world could not have explained what it was really like on those bicycles as we puffed and talked and laughed along the way.

In the same manner, understanding the theory of Christianity, even belonging to a church, can never for one moment give any indication of what it is really like to experience the love of Jesus by the power of the Holy Spirit in a converted Christian life. "But when the kindness and love of God our Savior toward man appeared, not by works of righteousness which we have done, but according to His mercy He saved us, through the washing of regeneration and renewing of the Holy Spirit, whom He poured out on us abundantly through Jesus Christ our Savior, that having been justified by His grace we should become heirs according to the hope of eternal life" (Titus 3:4-7).

"And the disciples were filled with joy and with the Holy Spirit" (Acts 13:52).

We began this chapter by asking the question "Where is the Holy Spirit in relationship to an unconverted life?" The answer is clear. Amazing Grace is a person, the person of the Holy Spirit. He is doing all that is possible in love to draw each unconverted soul to Jesus, offering the gift of repentance and salvation. We can even sleep at night knowing that while we rest the Holy Spirit does not for one moment relax His tireless efforts to bring every person into the kingdom of God.

Amazing Grace Is a Person

Cohesive Contrasts

Small groups have flourished for many centuries, as they have understood that our differences can draw us together rather than separate us. To get to know each person in your group a little better, share these two questions together:

1. What is one thing you enjoy doing without fear of failure?

2. What do you think has given you this confidence? For example, education, practice, natural talent, etc.

Consideration of the Word
Study text: Titus 2:11 to 3:7

Before you studied this chapter, what was your understanding of grace?

Unmerited favor _____ Blessing upon food _____

Dignity _____ Girl's name _____ Other _____

According to Titus 2:11, how many people have been influenced by God's grace?_____

Discuss some ways you see God accomplishing this._____

_____

Notice in Titus 2:11–14 that grace teaches, exalts Jesus, and explains salvation. In what ways does this remind you of the work of the Holy Spirit?_____

Notice Acts 4:31. How does the discovery that grace is the power of the Holy Spirit make you feel right now?

Surprised _____ Happy _____ Puzzled _____

Grateful _____ Strong _____ Other _____

Do you have a brief experience you would like to tell of God's grace working with you and leading you to conversion? Why not share it with the group, noticing differences between your experience and that of others? _____

_____

_____

_____

Read Titus 3:4. Paul speaks of the work of grace as the kindness and love of our Saviour. How can Christians be used to reveal God's kindness and love to those who may be unconverted?_____

_____

_____

As the Spirit of grace and supplication leads me to mourn that my sins crucified Jesus (Zechariah 12:10) I should—

Continue to feel depressed _____ Feel utterly worthless _____

Forget about it all _____ Move from sorrow to joy _____

Give God the glory _____ Be careful not to sin again _____

Be cautious of the Spirit _____ Other _____

Is there some special way that you have experienced the renewing power of the Holy Spirit in your life recently (Titus 3:5)? For instance, has there been renewed love, energy, trust, health, encouragement, etc.? _____

_____

_____

The grace of God working through the power of the Holy Spirit leads us to accept Jesus as Saviour. In this way we are justified—counted as if we have never sinned (verse 7). What connection can you see between this assurance and the joy of Spirit-filled New Testament Christians? _____

_____

Conversation With the Lord

Let each group member who feels comfortable interact in prayer with each other and the Lord.

First, pray brief prayers of praise.

Second, pray for the Spirit of grace and supplication, thanking God for the sacrifice of Jesus for our sins.

Finally, pray for specific needs in and outside the group.

Close the group meeting by praying the Lord's Prayer together.

Committing the Word to Memory

This week, write out Titus 3:4-6. Memorize these verses, then share them with someone as soon as possible._____

_____

_____

CHAPTER
THREE
▼

Taking Up Residence

Whith words like "born again" and "converted" are almost clichés of Christian jargon, they describe an event as real as human birth. None doubt their birth, although millions do not know why they were born. Many wish that they had not been born, and some teenagers are so serious about this that in each of the last years of the 1980s more than 500,000 teens in the United States attempted suicide.

However, in 25 years of ministry I cannot remember ever hearing of anyone seriously regretting opening his or her heart to Jesus. To experience that distinctly remarkable transformation of life that Jesus spoke of as the new birth is something that true Christians continue to look on with unspeakable awe.

"What happened when you were born again?" I asked a young man who was excited about his conversion experience. His answer was typical of what many Christians would say. "Jesus came into my life."

Limiting the Limitless One

This brings me to a question that can be a little disturbing. Can Jesus as a person really come into our lives? Think about this with me. When Jesus came to earth and accepted humanity, it appears that He voluntarily surrendered His omnipresence. On earth Jesus' power and thoughts could transcend distance. Remember how He knew about Nathanael (John 1:43-50) and how He could heal a person like the centurion's servant, who was not in His presence (Matthew 8:5-13)? Nevertheless, when Jesus was in Capernaum He was not in Jerusalem. When Lazarus died in Bethany, Mary and Martha mourned because Jesus was in another part of the country (John 11). Do you ever feel concerned that Jesus is in another part of the universe?

Apparently when Jesus ascended to heaven He retained His humanity with His limited omnipresence. The angels told His disciples that it would be the same Jesus who ascended who would return at the Second Coming (Acts 1:11). He would come then with the same flesh and bones that characterized Him as the risen Saviour (Luke 24:36-53). While Jesus certainly knows all of His people, He is voluntarily restricted, humanly speaking, to His ministry in the heavenly sanctuary, where He ever lives to make intercession for us (Hebrews 7:23-25).

If Jesus in His human form was on earth today, He could not be in the Colorado Rockies at the same time as accompanying a group of hikers in the beautiful Southern Alps of New Zealand. If He were on a flight from Amman to Rome, He could not at the same time escort you from San Francisco to Honolulu. Although this sort of reasoning may be rather simplistic, the implications are startling. Are we alone? Was Jesus wrong when He said He would be with us until the end of the world?

This apparently is one of the reasons that Jesus said, "It is to your advantage that I go away" (John 16:7). He explained this by saying that the Comforter would come in His name and dwell with His people forever (John 14:16, 26).

Recently I talked to a man who told me, with deep conviction, that he is the third person of the Godhead. When I expressed my skepticism, he reminded me that I was showing the same attitude to him as was shown to Jesus when He preached in His hometown of Nazareth. But there are qualities that the Holy Spirit is endowed with that this man can never possess. While the one claiming to be the Holy Spirit was in Washington, D.C., he could not be in Washington State. While he was riding the Metro train on the Silver Spring line, he was not walking the Mall. While he was in Arlington, he was not on an airliner. On the other hand, David, writing by inspiration of the Holy Spirit, says in Psalm 139, "Where can I go from Your Spirit? Or where can I flee from Your presence? If I ascend into heaven, You are there. If I make my bed in hell, behold, You are there. If I take the wings of the morning, and dwell in the uttermost parts of the sea, even there Your hand shall lead me, and Your right hand shall hold me. If I say, 'Surely the darkness shall fall on me,' even the night shall be light about me; indeed, the darkness shall not hide from You but the night shines as the day; the darkness and the light are both alike to You" (verses 7-12).

A Guest Moves In

Remember that Jesus said that the Holy Spirit "dwells with you and will be in you" (John 14:17). The question that puzzled me a few years ago was "When did the transition take place?" When did the Holy Spirit actually come into my life, and how did that relate to Paul's words, which clearly indicate that Jesus shall dwell in our hearts by faith (Ephesians 3:17)?

You may not have analyzed so technically the significance of being born again or may not particularly want to, but let me tell you how this understanding helped me. Babies apparently have no biological understanding of their entry into the world, but after a number of years most people learn some elementary principles of birth, and we are very glad that some people become midwives and obstetricians. I was helped by what you might call a spiritually obstetrical study of the relationship between the Holy Spirit and new birth.

Paul, in a very clear way, describes the moment of transition between when the Holy Spirit is *with* a person and when He comes *into* a person. Look at Ephesians 1:13: "In Him you also trusted, after you heard the word of truth, the gospel of your salvation; in whom also, having believed, you were sealed with the Holy Spirit of promise, who is the guarantee of our inheritance until the redemption of the purchased possession to the praise of His glory." Later on he says, "And do not grieve the Holy Spirit of God, by whom you were sealed for the day of redemption" (Ephesians 4:30). Paul believes that Christians have been sealed by the Spirit, and has clearly outlined how that takes place.

Ephesians 1:13 especially describes step by step the way of salvation. First, the Word is heard and trusted. Second, the gospel of salvation is understood, and third, the repentant sinner takes the step of faith.

In the rather secular city of Sydney I advertised a series of evangelistic meetings that began by showing the reliability of the Bible. A young high school teacher who claimed to be an atheist came to the meetings to find material to use when attacking Christianity in his science classes. To his amazement, he discovered that the Bible is actually reliable and trustworthy. History, archaeology, and prophecy combined with the moving of the Spirit upon Gordon's heart, and soon he was absorbed in the Word. As the gospel became clear, he accepted Jesus as his Saviour and was ultimately baptized.

This step-by-step experience has been repeated many times. After I began a series of lectures at the University of Idaho on the historical and archaeological accuracy of the prophecies of Daniel 2, more than a dozen students, including some completing Ph.D.s, came to trust the Word and accept the gospel and the fundamentals of faith. Finally, they followed through by being baptized in the name of the Father, Son, and Holy Spirit.

Apparently it is at the moment of new birth, or conversion, that the Holy Spirit comes to dwell in the newly opened heart. Paul says, "Having believed, you were sealed with the Holy Spirit of promise." This is called the "guarantee," which according to 2 Corinthians 5:5 is the gift of the Holy Spirit in a new believer's life.

Paul emphasizes this again in 2 Corinthians 1:21, 22, where he says, "Now He who establishes us with you in Christ and has anointed us is God, who also has sealed us and given us the Spirit in our hearts as a deposit." Notice the word "deposit" here. This is the same word translated "guarantee" in 2 Corinthians 5:5 and Ephesians 1:14. In the King James Version the word is "earnest," which, according to Strong, is the purchase money given in advance as a security for the rest. When I purchased a house in Oregon, the realtor required a $1,000 earnest money, which he retained as a guarantee that all the rest of the same money would follow in due time. It's taking me 30 years to fulfill what I promised by the earnest money.

The Holy Spirit, given into my life at conversion, is not only God's seal of ownership upon me so I can truly take the name Christian, but God's assurance to me that eventually I will receive completely all that God has for me in eternity. It is the guarantee, Paul says, of the purchased possession.

I used to speak as if some people were converted Christians yet did not have the Holy Spirit in their lives. Now I receive tremendous courage from knowing that every born-again Christian is a dwelling place of the Spirit. "Do you not know that your body is the temple of the Holy Spirit who is in you, whom you have from God and you are not your own? For you were bought at a price; therefore glorify God in your body and in your spirit, which are God's" (1 Corinthians 6:19, 20). That is why Paul could say that those who do not have the Holy Spirit do not even belong to Jesus (Romans 8:9).

Recently a friend of mine shared a statement with me that increased my courage even further. "To all who have accepted Christ as a personal Saviour, the Holy Spirit has come as a counselor, sanctifier, guide, and witness." [1] This means that the power within each Christian is incredible. To use an auto age illustration, we could say that we have an engine within us that has vast resources of "horsepower" just waiting to be used.

When she was about 16, our daughter, Sharon, fell in love with Corvettes. Whenever she saw one of these powerful sports cars on the road, she would point it out with great enthusiasm. One day as we drove to our local supermarket she let out a piercing scream. I jammed on the brakes, thinking we were about to be involved in a dreadful accident. "Look at that," she shouted, pointing to a red Corvette being driven slowly along the road by a little old gray-haired lady. "What a waste! All of that power, and the old lady driving it just putts along! Has she borrowed the car from her grandson?" Imagine what would happen if the lady pushed the accelerator to the floor. The tires would scream and smoke, the engine would roar, and hopefully the traffic would part before her like the waters of the Red Sea.

The potential of power available within the Christian life is limited only by the degree of our surrender to God.

With the Guest Comes the Rest

Sometimes this power that comes into a Christian life at conversion has been called Trinity Power. I was amazed to find in John 14:16-23, after He had promised that His Holy Spirit would dwell in His disciples, Jesus then stated that in this way He Himself would come into them. So with the coming of the Holy Spirit, the Christian has within him the Spirit and the Son. Speaking of Jesus' disciples, Dutch Reformed pastor Andrew Murray says, "In the Holy Spirit He came as the indwelling Christ, to become in the very innermost recesses of their being the life of their life. . . . Jesus, whom they had known in His earthly ministry, they now received by the Spirit in His heavenly glory within them."[2]

But there is more. Jesus, in John 14, goes on to talk of the Father, and then using the plural, He says of the Christian, "We will come to him and make Our home with him." Just as in Jesus dwelt all the fullness of the Godhead bodily, so the born-again Christian is made a habitation of God in the Spirit, just as is the household of God (Ephesians 2:22). The presence of the Holy Spirit is counted also as the presence of the Father and the Son.

Most people when they become born-again Christians know very little about the Holy Spirit. I certainly knew almost nothing about Him. My knowledge of the Holy Spirit was limited to the basic formula of "Father, Son, and Holy Spirit," who comprised, I was told, the Godhead, or the God family. The three beings, equal within the Godhead, were called the Trinity, or the Tri-unity. Who or what the Holy Spirit is I did not know, but even so the Holy Spirit had worked to lead me to accept Jesus as my Saviour and to invite Jesus into my heart. It was this conversion experience that actually brought the Holy Spirit into my life.

It was the Spirit in my life right at conversion that enabled me actually to have assurance that I had received eternal life at the moment I accepted Jesus. "By this we know that we abide in Him, and He in us, because He has given us of His Spirit" (1 John 4:13). "And this is the testimony: that God has given us eternal life, and this life is in His Son. He who has the Son has life; and he who does not have the Son of God does not have life. These things I have written to you who believe in the name of the Son of God, that you may know that you have eternal life, and that you may continue to believe in the name of the Son of God" (1 John 5:11-13).

If you have accepted Jesus as your Saviour, isn't it exciting to know that you have *now* the assurance of salvation and eternal life? The Holy Spirit glorifies, in your heart and mind, the wonderful Saviour whose death on the cross made possible your forgiveness and daily victory. Praise God for the Spirit, who is in your life right now! You are never alone, because through the Spirit, Jesus is with you until the end of the world. Talk to Him. Thank Him. Praise His name.

Taking Up Residence

Cohesive Contrasts

Here are two "getting to know each other" questions for this group meeting:

1. What house have you enjoyed living in most, and why was it special to you?

2. If you could build a special house for Jesus somewhere on earth what would it be like? Why do you think He would be pleased with it?

Consideration of the Word
Study Text: John 14:16-24

Jesus seems to indicate that it is better for us that He returned to heaven rather than stay on earth (John 16:7). How would you feel if He lived on your street right now?

Safe _____ Embarrassed _____ Frightened _____ Concerned when He is away _____ Wishing He was in another part of the world _____ Other _____

Although Jesus voluntarily limited His ability to be everywhere at once, how do you see the Holy Spirit making up for this (Psalm 139:7-12)?_____

_____

_____

Read Romans 8:9. How definite is Paul about Christians having the Holy Spirit in their lives?_____

_____

Jesus promised that the Holy Spirit will come into the lives of certain people (John 14:17). To whom does this happen and what steps make it possible, according to Ephesians 1:13?_____

_____

_____

How do you feel about the Holy Spirit actually dwelling in you as a born-again Christian?

Puzzled _____   Nervous _____   Honored _____

Excited _____   Cautious _____   Surprised _____

Other _____

Have you ever paid a deposit or down payment on an expensive item? What does it mean to you that Jesus at your conversion gives you the Holy Spirit as a down payment, or guarantee, of all that He has for you in heaven (Ephesians 1:14)? _____

_____

_____

_____

The Father sends the Holy Spirit in Jesus' name (John 14:26). Explain in your own words the connection you see between this and Jesus' being represented in us by the Holy Spirit (verse 18)._____

_____

_____

What does "We" and "Our" in John 14:23 mean to you in the light of the special unity of the Father, Son, and Holy Spirit?_____

_____

Through the Spirit we "know" we have eternal life (1 John 5:11-13). We "know" God lives in us (1 John 4:13). Discuss this assurance of salvation. What does it mean to you as a Christian? Is it right to be certain about eternal life? How can this assurance be explained in such a way that an unconverted person will want it?_____

_____

_____

_____

Conversation With the Lord

The group that prays together stays together. Make prayer a most important part of your group interaction.

First, adore God; praise Him for who He is—a God of love.

Second, pray that all group members will have opened their lives to be a dwelling place of the Holy Spirit; then include others outside the group in this special prayer.

Third, pray that the Lord will use you to bring the assurance of salvation to someone the Lord may lead you to this week.

Close as usual with the Lord's Prayer.

Committing the Word to Memory

This week, write out John 14:16, 17. Memorize these verses, then share them with someone as soon as possible.

_____

_____

CHAPTER FOUR

The Identity Crisis

Have you ever tried to become acquainted with an influence or power? It is rather difficult. It is impersonal. "Let me introduce you to magnetism," my science teacher said. "Let us see how it works and how we can use it." My wife, Barbara, has collected refrigerator magnets for 20 years, and her international collection is now worth more than our refrigerator. But the magnets have no personal concern for us. I have used a magnet on a piece of string to fish a small bolt out of an awkward place in a car engine. It worked, and I appreciated it.

Many people think of the Holy Spirit in much the same way as magnetism or electricity. "How can I get it? How can I use it?" The Bible is abundantly clear, however, that the Holy Spirit is a person as real as the Father and the Son. The great evangelist D. L. Moody once wrote, "I was a Christian a long time before I found out that the Holy Ghost was a person. Now, this is something a great many don't seem to understand, but if you will just take up the Bible and see what Christ had to say about the Holy Spirit, you will find that He always spoke of Him as a person. He never spoke of Him as an influence." [1]

Jesus' use of personal pronouns regarding the Holy Spirit are strikingly significant. Notice nine of them in these two verses. "However, when He, the Spirit of truth, has come, He will guide you into all truth; for He will not speak on His own authority, but whatever He hears He will speak; and He will tell you things to come. He will glorify Me, for He will take of what is Mine and declare it to you" (John 16:13, 14).

Use It or Use Us?

Whenever the Holy Spirit is thought of as a power or influence, people are inclined to try to manipulate that power for their own purposes. I must admit that there have been times when I have prayed for power to do some seemingly important work of mine rather than asking for an openness to the awareness of the presence of the Holy Spirit within me. Not only does He give power, but with Him will come all else that I need.

The Holy Spirit is often thought of in an impersonal way, just as people sometimes think of the church. A man on one occasion called our church secretary and asked for the pastor. When I answered the phone, he began to attack the church and say it owed him money. In fact, he wanted some offering money returned that he had given to the church years before. I explained to him that the church is neither a building nor a denomination, but people. "Would you like to meet the people and ask them for the money?" I queried. "If you are to get money from the church, it will have to be their money."

"No," he exclaimed, "I don't want it from the people. I want it from the church."

Similarly, people believe that God owes them something. They do not want God, but they want His help, His power. To get to know the church, we must get to know people. To get God's power, we must get to know a Person.

Simon, in ancient Samaria, thought he could purchase the power of the Holy Spirit with money (Acts 8:18-22). Some today would try to purchase Holy Spirit power with ambitious plans and programs that are supposedly to give God glory but rather can be a revelation of human power and a heart not right in the sight of God (verse 21). Years ago I underlined these words in *The Desire of Ages:* "We cannot use the Holy Spirit. The Holy Spirit is to use us." [2]

In Holy Spirit seminars in North America and overseas I found that many people can quote those words, but few know the context. When I noticed them again recently, the context really challenged me. "There are many who believe and profess to claim the Lord's promise; they talk *about* Christ and *about* the Holy Spirit, yet receive no benefit. They do not surrender the soul to be guided and controlled by the divine agencies. We cannot use the Holy Spirit. The Spirit is to use us. Through the Spirit God works in His people 'to will and to do of his good pleasure' (Philippians 2:13, KJV). But many will not submit to this. They want to manage themselves. This is why they do not receive the heavenly gift." [3]

Not only is the Holy Spirit spoken of in Scripture as a person, but some of His personal qualities are mentioned describing activities that are usually accomplished only by people. The Spirit searches (1 Corinthians 2:10), knows (verse 11), teaches (verse 13), gives gifts as He wills (1 Corinthians 12:7-11). He loves (Romans 15:30), He can speak (Acts

8:29), He can be lied to (Acts 5:3, 4). The Holy Spirit can be grieved (Ephesians 4:30) and even insulted (Matthew 12:31).

In a talk she gave to the students at Avondale College Adventist pioneer Ellen White said, "We need to realize that the Holy Spirit, who is as much a person as God is a person, is walking through these grounds." [4] In *The Desire of Ages*, which was completed about the same time as that statement was made, the same speaker writes, "The Holy Spirit is Christ's representative, but divested of the personality of humanity, and independent thereof. Cumbered with humanity, Christ could not be in every place personally. Therefore it was for their interest that He should go to the Father, and send the Spirit to be His successor on earth. No one could then have an advantage because of his location or his personal contact with Christ. By the Spirit the Saviour would be accessible to all. In this sense He would be nearer to them than if He had not ascended on high." [5] While the latter part of this statement supports our discussion of omnipresence in the previous chapter, the first part presents an interesting perspective of the Spirit. While He is a person as real as you or your mother, He does not have the personality of humanity. This makes the Holy Spirit harder to comprehend and visualize than the Father and the Son, for we are used to creating God in our own image. The Scriptures are clear, however, that the Holy Spirit is as much a person as the other two in the heavenly Trio.

He Is Good; but Is He God?

Once I became aware that the Holy Spirit is a person I wondered, What kind of person is He? Who is He? When a person runs for the presidency of the United States today, his whole life comes under the closest scrutiny. Will he pass the test of the media bloodhounds who will search out the credibility and morality of every facet of his life? When we examine the Holy Spirit, who is called "searcher of heart and mind," what do we find? Let's look at the credentials of the One who took up residence in our life at conversion.

It is significant to discover that the Holy Spirit takes a submissive role to the other two members of the Trinity. Just as Jesus said He came not to do His own will, but the will of Him who sent Him (John 6:38), so the Holy Spirit, in coming to minister to and through God's people, was also sent. "But when the Helper comes, whom I shall send to you from the Father, the Spirit of truth who proceeds from the Father, He will testify of Me" (John 15:26).

Interestingly enough, it was this text that finally caused the split between the Eastern and Western Orthodox churches in 1054. The original creed of the early Christian churches known as the Nicene Creed (A.D. 325) stated that the Holy Spirit had proceeded from the Father. A later copyist's error apparently slipped in the phrase that the Holy Spirit had proceeded from the Father and the Son. The Eastern Orthodox churches refused to accept this statement, but they do see the Scriptures plainly emphasizing that the Holy Spirit is not only the Spirit of the Father, but also of the Son, Jesus (Romans 8:9; Philippians 1:19; 1 Peter 1:11; John 20:22; Acts 2:33).

Clearly the Bible teaches that the Holy Spirit is God, or as we say, part of the Trinity. The equality of the Holy Spirit within the Trinity is indicated by the baptismal formula "In the name (singular) of the Father and of the Son and of the Holy Spirit" (Matthew 28:19). Apparently the name God can be likened to a family name, so we say, "God the Father, God the Son, and God the Holy Spirit."

In the story of Ananias and Sapphira, Peter emphasized that when they lied to the Holy Spirit, they actually lied to God (Acts 5:1-4, 9). The Father, Son, and Holy Spirit are so closely united as one God that it is said, "God is Spirit" (John 4:24) and "the Lord is the Spirit" (2 Corinthians 3:17). The qualities of the Holy Spirit such as omnipresence and omnipotence are actually distinctives of God.

Now, we have waded through all this so we can come to a most joyful realization. The Holy Spirit within us as born-again Christians is in reality God within us. Hallelujah! I do not have just the power of God in me—I have God in me. As a friend of mine says, "God is resident and president" when I am fully open to the Spirit.

I like the way Samuel Chadwick illustrates this closeness as he speaks of the incarnation of the Spirit. "The marginal reading of Judges 6:34 (RV) will help us here again, especially if we read it in the light of New Testament experience: 'The Spirit clothed Himself with Gideon.' Spirit clothing itself with humanity is the miracle of the Incarnation. A body is as necessary to the Spirit as to the Son. For the Son a Body was prepared by the Spirit; for the Spirit a Body is made possible by the Son. The Spirit lived in and through Gideon. The life of Gideon became the life of the Spirit. The man was endued and the Spirit was clothed. The Spirit thought through Gideon's brain, felt through Gideon's heart, looked through Gideon's eyes, spake through Gideon's voice, wrought by Gideon's hands, and yet all the time Gideon was still Gideon and the Spirit was still the Spirit." [6]

The Holy Spirit does not enter us at the time of conversion using the tactics of a viscious coup d'état, but in love as a friend or a spouse on a happy wedding day. In fact, "the love of God has been poured out in our hearts by the Holy Spirit who was given to us" (Romans 5:5). The relationship we have with the Spirit who dwells in us can be more intimate and meaningful than any other relationship on earth. Paul speaks of this as the "fellowship of the Spirit" (Philippians 2:1).

Friendship and Fellowship

If you have accepted Jesus as your Saviour and thus become the dwelling place of the Holy Spirit, are you really spending time fellowshipping with Him? Through prayer and meditation on God's Word, we really have a beautiful association with the Holy Spirit. A friendship develops that is as strong as epoxy glue.

Across the hallway from my office is the women's ministries center, where Ruthie Jacobsen is the director. Ruthie, the conference president's wife and former nursing administrator, has been used of God in many special and marvelous ways. She has had the opportunity of sharing the power of God with pastors and lay leaders. Many times Ruthie has told me of remarkable answers to her prayers of faith. Her prayers have raised thousands of dollars for ministry, and her retreats for church leaders and women's groups have blessed hundreds. But what impressed me most about Ruthie was a quiet confidence that indicated a special fellowship with the Holy Spirit. I discovered accidentally how important that fellowship with the Spirit is to Ruthie when her husband, Don, one day mentioned to me that she had been up at 4:30 a.m. praying. Was this a once-in-a-lifetime event? No, it is the regular pattern of her life.

Recently I heard Ruthie tell a group of pastors and their spouses how the Holy Spirit had convicted her of a certain sin as she had fellowshipped with Him in the early morning. Surprisingly, the Spirit also convicted her to share that sin with those who attended the meeting. What a struggle! "Who would want to hear about it? What will they think of me?" Years of daily fellowship with the Spirit have given Ruthie an obedient heart. Eyes filled with tears as she told the story. The sin was not great by worldly standards, but sin is sin in the eyes of God. Her willingness to listen to the voice of the Spirit and share led many others, myself included, to confess their faults to one another and to pray for one another.

In communion with the Spirit it becomes increasingly possible to recognize the voice of God. As I was driving a few days ago, I listened to

45

a number of cassette tapes from workshops at a small group conference. Often questions were asked and sometimes I would immediately recognize a voice. *Listen to this question from Alphonso McCarthy,* I thought as the group discussed with Don Jacobsen some aspect of Bible study preparation. I had known Pastor McCarthy for eight years. We had shared together in ministry. His voice was unmistakable.

Jesus said, "My sheep know My voice" (see John 10:1-16). God's voice is heard through the appeals of the Holy Spirit making impressions upon the heart.[7] How can I know the difference between my own imaginations and the impressions of the Holy Spirit? Only through daily fellowship with Him.

Once I began to spend an hour in prayer each day really communicating with God and praying in the Spirit (Jude 20), allowing the Spirit to intercede with me through groanings that cannot be uttered (Romans 8:26, 27), I began to be led by the Spirit as never before (verse 14). Out of this grew the Homes of Hope Small Group Ministry, *Window to Revelation* study guides, Trinity Power Ministry, Holy Spirit Fellowships, and International Small Group and Prayer Conferences. These have dramatically affected the lives of thousands and impacted whole churches, but the praise and honor goes to God, not man. I am deeply convicted that by fellowship with God who dwells in us, we can be used as His servants in a way we could never possibly visualize without the presence of His person resident and president in our hearts.

As you fellowship with the Holy Spirit today, talk to Him. You may be used to having fellowship with the Father and the Son (1 John 1:3). As you now begin to fellowship also with the Spirit, tell Him you love Him and that you appreciate His ministry in your life. As Paul writes about fellowship or communion with the Spirit, he twice uses the word *koinania* (Philippians 2:1; 2 Corinthians 13:14), which means communication and partnership. Daily communication with the Holy Spirit, listening to the voice of God, will lead you into partnership with Him. Some pastors have said that the Holy Spirit is their senior pastor. A ministry team like that is powerful to the glory of God. In partnership with the Holy Spirit He will open the possibilities for ministry beyond anything we can ever imagine. Not only that, but through fellowship with the Holy Spirit, we can have a partnership that can be victorious against all evil from without or within. Now, that is something to sing about!

The Identity Crisis

Cohesive Contrasts

By now your group will be bonding together. New people joining the group will quickly sense the fellowship and trust. Here is your "getting to know you" question:

How do you deal with unidentified people who talk to you on the phone expecting you will recognize their voice? Tell of voices you recognize most readily.

Consideration of the Word
Study Text: John 16:7-15

Previous to this study, what word would best describe your understanding of who or what is the Holy Spirit?

Ghost _____   Influence _____   Power _____

Man _____   Woman _____   Spirit _____

God _____   Person _____   Don't know _____

Conscience _____   Energy _____   Other _____

What significance do you see in Jesus' use of the personal pronouns "He, Him, His" 12 times in our study text? _____

_____

_____

List some differences it makes to our relationship to the Holy Spirit when we think of Him as a person rather than an impersonal power. _____

_____

_____

_____

Read John 16:7-14 and name some of the specific attributes of a person that Jesus applies to the Holy Spirit (e.g., "guides"). _____

_____

_____

_____

What evidence of the unity between the Father, Son, and Holy Spirit do you see in Matthew 28:19, 20? _____

_____

_____

Understanding that the Holy Spirit is an actual person who dwells within you, how can you best relate to Him?

Ignore Him _____ Occasionally recognize Him _____

Say hello once each week _____ Develop a friendship with Him _____

Have a constant fellowship with Him _____ Other _____

How long does it take you to get to know a stranger? How do you go about it?

_____

_____

The Holy Spirit speaks to Christians and tells them things (John 16:13). How do you see this happening through Bible study and prayer? Has God ever spoken to you through a verse of Scripture? What happened? _____

_____

_____

_____

The Holy Spirit leads people into deeply earnest prayer (Romans 8:26, 27), which is sometimes called praying in the Spirit (Jude 20). This usually takes some time with God in prayer. Do you have an experience of fervent prayer that was followed by a special answer you would like to share? _____

_____

_____

_____

Read Romans 5:5. What are some ways you have seen the Holy Spirit pouring the love of God into your heart? What took place? _____

_____

_____

Conversation With the Lord

Perhaps you would like to sing some prayer songs in your group if this has not happened yet.

First, pray or sing prayers of thanksgiving to God.

Second, pray for fellowship with the Holy Spirit and that each person in the group will know and love the Holy Spirit.

Third, pray for special needs in the group and outside the group. Pray that

God will bring others to join the group.

Conclude as usual by praying the Lord's Prayer together.

Committing the Word to Memory

This week, write out John 16:13. Memorize this verse, then share it with someone as soon as possible.

_____

_____

_____

_____

Conscious of His Coming

Some Christians are "feelings" orientated, and others are "feelings" dislocated. For some, exuberant feelings are the goal and pinnacle of Christianity. For others, joyful feelings are as rare as squirrels in the Sahara.

"I do not believe that Christianity or even the filling of Christians by the Holy Spirit should be based on feelings," a man said to me recently in a rather negative tone of voice. I agreed with him as far as the word "based" is concerned, understanding the preeminence of facts and faith. However, there is no doubt that facts and faith have their fruitage in positive feelings that gently fill the heart and sometimes explode in the life of a Spirit-filled Christian. "For the kingdom of God is not food and drink, but righteousness and peace and joy in the Holy Spirit" (Romans 14:17).

Usually when a Christian life is gripped by fear, doubt, discouragement, and even depression, it is important to consider facts and faith prayerfully. It is no doubt true also that when a Christian life is filled with negativism, criticism, and unresolved anger, it is necessary again to examine the facts and faith.

Feelings, Faith, and Filling

It is significant to notice that there is a very definite interplay between feelings and faith when it comes to understanding the baptism and the filling of the Holy Spirit. Just as love is more than a knowledge of hormones, so the filling of a life by the Holy Spirit is more than an understanding of texts. But it was "texts" that first made me aware of the possibility of the deep movings of the Holy Spirit in my heart and life.

Although Paul confirmed that the Ephesians had been sealed by the Spirit (Ephesians 1:13; 4:30), he went on to admonish them to be "filled with the Spirit" (Ephesians 5:18). Jesus had breathed on His disiciples and given them the Holy Spirit (John 20:22), but had later told them that they would be baptized with the Spirit (Acts 1:5). This baptism of the Spirit happened when they were filled with the Spirit 40 days later (Acts 2:4). The baptism or filling of the Holy Spirit is also spoken of as the Spirit being poured out (verse 33) and "coming upon" (Acts 19:6). The most common term, though, is simply "filled with the Spirit." You will find this numerous times in the New Testament.

The potential of what God has for His people is beyond what we can ever imagine even at conversion. The experience of John Wesley has really helped me to understand some of the things that I have seen in my own path of spiritual growth. You may remember that John Wesley was an Anglican clergyman who was one of the founders of the Holy Club at Oxford University in the early part of the eighteenth century. Wesley's one aim, he told his father, was to secure personal holiness. Because of the methodical way John Wesley and his small group at Oxford went about this pursuit of holiness, they became known as Methodists, a term used in derision initially, although later it became the respected title of the denomination Wesley founded. Out of the later Wesleyan movement grew such dedicated Christian groups as the Church of the Nazarene.

At the time of the Holy Club there was one major problem. Wesley and his friends did not understand conversion. After he returned from a short and unfruitful experience as a missionary to the American Indians he wrote in his diary, "I went to America to convert the Indians, but who will convert me?" Back in England on Wednesday, May 24, 1738, he finally "broke the faith barrier." Here is the famous entry from John Wesley's diary: "In the evening I went very unwillingly to a society on Aldersgate Street, where one was reading Luther's preface to the Epistle to the Romans. About a quarter before nine, while he was describing the change which God works in the heart through faith in Christ, I felt my heart strangely warmed. I felt I did trust in Christ, Christ alone for salvation: and an assurance was given me, that He had taken *my* sins, even *mine,* and saved *me* from the law of sin and death."

Some time ago in a church seminar I was telling of John Wesley's experience. We spoke for some time about the significance of a heart that is strangely warmed. While returning home that evening, a small girl asked her father what it meant to have a heart that was strangely warmed. The father tried to explain the joy and peace that comes into the life that has accepted Jesus and His forgiveness personally and sincerely. About a half hour after returning home, the little girl came from her bedroom and explained to her father with great joy, "While I was saying my prayers tonight, I asked Jesus to come into my life, and Daddy, as I prayed, my heart was strangely warmed."

A heart that is strangely warmed is a definite and beautiful feeling. Yet two days after Wesley experienced this in the Aldersgate Chapel he records that he was still "in heaviness because of manifold temptations." Wesley's awareness of the complete filling with the Holy Spirit was evident seven months later during an all-night prayer meeting in the Moravian Chapel on Fetter Lane, London. George Whitefield's biographer tells the experience that involves John Wesley on January 1, 1739: "This love feast at Fetter Lane was a memorial one. Besides about 60 Moravians who were present, not fewer than seven of the Oxford Methodists, namely John and Charles Wesley, George Whitefield, Westley Hall, Benjamin Binghall, Charles Kinchin, and Richard Hopkins, all of them were ordained clergymen of the Church of England." Wesley writes, "About three in the morning, as we were continuing instant in prayer, the power of God came mightily upon us, insomuch that many cried for exceeding joy, and many fell to the ground. As soon as we were recovered a little from that awe and amazement at the presence of His Majesty, we broke out with one voice, 'We praise Thee, O God; we acknowledge Thee to be the Lord.' "

In the library at Andrews University I surveyed more than 350 books on the subject of the Holy Spirit. Authors of most denominations have written on this topic, although the Holy Spirit has often been pushed into the background behind theological debates and denominational indoctrination. One of the earliest Adventist books on the Holy Spirit in the Andrews library was written by J. H. Waggoner and published by the old steam press in Battle Creek, Michigan, in 1877. I like Waggoner's emphasis as he differentiates between water baptism and the baptism of the Holy Spirit. "In all cases where [water] baptism is taken as the evidence of the gift of the Spirit, the professing penitent is lulled into carnal security, trusting solely to his baptism as the evidence of his favor with God. Baptism, not the Spirit in the heart, becomes his *earnest* or *witness.* . . . Whether received before or after [water] baptism, it is shown that the gift of the Spirit was not then considered a matter of course because of [water] baptism; but was a matter of personal conscious experience." [1] Notice Waggoner believes that the baptism of the Holy Spirit will involve a "personal conscious experience."

When you have a conscious experience, you know what is happening.

Fact and feeling are intermingled. A man fainted during his wedding ceremony. Although friends videoed the whole scene, the groom was unconscious of all that took place. However, to the embarrassed bride who tried to stop him from sliding to the floor, it was a very conscious experience.

What conscious experience precedes and accompanies the filling of the Holy Spirit?

A Thirst for More

First, it seems that there is created in the heart a deep thirsting, a longing. This longing involves a desire to be like Jesus, to serve Him. It is a longing to know God and be fully surrendered to Him. Notice how the psalmist expressed this so graphically. "As the deer pants for the water brooks, so pants my soul for You, O God. My soul thirsts for God, for the living God. When shall I come and appear before God?" (Psalm 42:1, 2). "O God, You are my God; early will I seek You; my soul thirsts for You; my flesh longs for You in a dry and thirsty land where there is no water. So I have looked for You in the sanctuary, to see Your power and Your glory" (Psalm 63:1, 2). "I spread out my hands to You; my soul longs for You like a thirsty land" (Psalm 143:6).

It is so easy to spend a fleeting moment in prayer and then wonder why there is a lack of power in our Christian life. The Bible indicates a deep earnestness in the daily relationship with God. A Christian who knew God intimately spoke of it in this way: "I saw how this grace could be obtained. Go to your closet, and there alone plead with God: 'Create in me a clean heart, O God; and renew a right spirit within me.' Be in earnest, be sincere. Fervent prayer availeth much. Jacoblike, wrestle in prayer. Agonize. Jesus, in the garden, sweat great drops of blood; you must make an effort. Do not leave your closet until you feel strong in God. . . . Come with zeal, and when you sincerely feel that without the help of God you perish, when you pant after Him as the hart panteth after the water brooks, then will the Lord strengthen you speedily. Then will your peace pass all understanding. If you expect salvation, you must pray. Take time. Be not hurried and careless in your prayers. Beg of God to work in you a thorough reformation, that the fruits of His Spirit may dwell in you, and you shine as lights in the world. . . . I saw that it is the privilege of every Christian to enjoy the deep movings of the Spirit of God." [2]

Because our minds are so clouded by the mass of negative influence of what surrounds us on television, radio, newspapers, magazines, and billboards, it seems difficult for a Christian initially to come to the place where there is a deep heart longing daily for God and His power. This same Christian leader writes, "Let all seek for the outpouring of the Holy Spirit. As with the disciples after the ascension of Christ, it may require several days of earnestly seeking God and putting away of sin." [3]

As a young Methodist, 15-year-old Ellen Harmon (who later became Ellen White), in the midst of her youthful Christian experience, was engulfed with feelings of deep sorrow and longed to understand more fully the love of God. In perplexity she visited Levi Stockman, a 30-year-old Methodist clergyman known for his genuine devotion to Christ. She records in her *Life Sketches* that he explained that "the very agony of mind I had suffered was positive evidence that the Spirit of the Lord was striving with me." Later he said, "Go free, Ellen. Return to your home trusting in Jesus, for He will not withhold His love from any true seeker." That evening Ellen experienced the certainty of the Holy Spirit filling her life. "As I prayed, the burden and agony of soul that I had so long endured left me and the blessing of the Lord descended upon me like the gentle dew. I praised God from the depths of my heart. Everything seemed shut out from me but Jesus and His glory, and I lost consciousness of what was passing around me. The Spirit of God rested upon me with such power that I was unable to go home that night." [4]

The Holy Spirit working on a Christian's heart and mind creates a thirsting and longing for God and His perfect righteousness. This longing deepens and intensifies, and the Spirit-filled Christian life grows into a more intimate daily relationship with God. Not understanding this, many Christians settle for a shallow relationship with God—a relationship that is predictable and routine. Even a tiny taste of the "living Water" of the Holy Spirit will create a thirst that will daily seek satisfaction by longing for more and more.

A few years ago, at a most inopportune moment, I was afflicted with a kidney stone. "Stone" sounds impressive, but it was in reality no more than a tiny grain of sand. When that particle of calcium finally passed, the urologist began to look for the reason that I had been smitten with this vicious affliction. Nothing in my diet seemed to provide the answer until he inquired about my water drinking habits. "I drink very little water," I explained, "because I rarely get thirsty." Now, you can guess what happened. For days I seemed to be floating in water. My whole family joined in encouraging me to drink, drink, drink. After a few weeks something amazing happened. I started to get thirsty. Now, as I drink a lot of water regularly, I always seem to be thirsty for more. The psalmist thirsted like that for daily supplies of the Living Water. So did Jesus. From nights in prayer He came forth each morning filled with the Spirit of God. I ministered for 15 years without much spiritual thirst. But now I come before God each day thirsting and longing to be filled with the Holy Spirit. This thirst for God and His righteousness, although based on the facts of God's Word, is as real as the thirst I experienced as a teenager after a hot day of throwing bales of hay on the back of a truck.

Ellen Harmon, the young Methodist girl who later became an Adventist pioneer, wrote toward the end of her fruitful life: "Plead for the Holy Spirit. God stands back of every promise He has made. With your Bible in your hands say, I have done as Thou hast said. I present Thy promise, 'Ask, and it shall be given you; seek, and ye shall find; knock, and it shall be opened unto you.' We must not only pray in Christ's name, but by the inspiration of the Holy Spirit. This explains what is meant when it is said that the Spirit 'maketh intercession for us with groanings which cannot be uttered' (Romans 8:26, KJV). Such prayer God delights to answer. When with earnestness and intensity we breathe a prayer in the name of Christ, there is in that very intensity a pledge from God that He is about to answer our prayer 'exceeding abundantly above all that we ask or think' (Ephesians 3:20)." [5]

We plead with God not because He is unwilling to answer, but because of the earnestness that springs up in our hearts for the filling of the Holy Spirit. Please remember that the deep longing is an indication that the Holy Spirit is moving in your heart and that God is about to answer your prayer.

Previous to the outpouring of the Holy Spirit on the festival day of Pentecost in Jerusalem, Jesus' disciples were "with one accord in prayer and supplication" (Acts 1:14). Before many new believers were filled with the Holy Spirit, they were "cut to the heart" and cried out "What shall we do?" (Acts 2:37). Prior to the shaking of the house of Peter and John's companions they raised their voices to God in earnest prayer (Acts 4:24-31). In Luke 11, before Jesus explained the asking, seeking, and knocking for the Holy Spirit, He told the story of the man who persistently and earnestly sought bread in the middle of the night (verses 5-13).

The Transforming Transition

Now, you might wonder how the transition comes between intense longing and thirsting and the awareness of being filled with the Spirit. The answer can only be "by faith." It is not because some exciting feeling grips the heart or mind, but because in the midst of the deep longing the Holy Spirit somehow indicates when, and enables the Christian to take the step of faith. The step of faith is taken when I say without any real initial proof, "Thank You, Lord, for filling me with Your Holy Spirit right now." I have claimed such promises as Luke 11:13: "If you then, being evil, know how to give good gifts to your children, how much more will your heavenly Father give the Holy Spirit to those who ask Him!" And because I believe God has heard and answered, I thank Him by faith. Paul emphasized this when he said, ". . . that we might receive the promise of the Spirit through faith" (Galatians 3:14). In fact, he already asked the rhetorical question in verse 2, "Did you receive the Spirit by the works of the law or by the hearing of faith?" Isaiah prophesied, "The Spirit is poured upon us from on high, and the wilderness becomes a fruitful field, and the fruitful field is counted as a forest. . . . The work of righteousness will be peace, and the effect of righteousness, quietness and assurance forever" (Isaiah 32:15-17).

Not only is the daily longing and thirsting for the Holy Spirit a conscious experience (to use Waggoner's term again), but so also is the result of the step of faith. Knowing the filling of the Holy Spirit is a conscious experience as well. Love wells up inside (Romans 5:5), praise replaces the spirit of heaviness (Isaiah 61:3), hope begins to fill the mind (Romans 15:13), a song makes music in the heart (Ephesians 5:18, 19).

Some days these feelings may be joyful and exuberant. Other days when you have a touch of the flu, your pet cat is lost, and your car has a flat tire, your feelings may be more muted. Nevertheless, there will be a firm belief that God has fulfilled His promise, that His word is true, and that you are a child of the King of heaven. As we will notice later this certainty can be called the inner witness of the Spirit.

Listen with me to a young pastor as he explains his experience with the Holy Spirit. Having attended a Holy Spirit Fellowship retreat, Ralph said, "I had never learned to pray, and my prayers were as scarce as oases in the desert. As I drove home I felt confused and angry about my confusion and then incredibly guilty because of my anger. A good pastor never resists praying and praising. It felt like a war was raging within me. I pleaded with God to clear the cloud and make some sense of my vexation. By the time I reached home, however, some pieces (and peace) began falling in place. That night I knelt with the psalmist and confessed, 'The sacrifices of God are a broken spirit, a broken and contrite heart—these, O God, You will not despise' [Psalm 51:17]."

Now Ralph goes on to describe what happened as he stopped saying maybe to God and simply opened his heart and said yes. "Others have spoken of peace, I've craved it myself, but I always thought it must be reserved for others born with more 'saint' in their bloodstream. It is hard to concede that our sainthood must always be based on Jesus' bloodstream. Personal devotions had also been an illusive goal. I justified it by sermon study time, telling myself I was getting to know God that way. I wasn't, and now I was thirsty. I recalled Jesus' words, 'Blessed are those who hunger and thirst for righteousness, for they shall be filled' [Matthew 5:6]. I was hungry now, but I wanted to be hungry consistently and be filled just as consistently. I pleaded with God to give me a daily hungering and thirst, but confidence grows shaky after years of Bible reading plan assaults, only to bail out in Leviticus or Numbers. He answers prayer. I still marvel, for I'm hungry and thirsty daily and am being filled. The Word of God, instead of merely being a parts bin from which I assemble suitable sermons, has become a companion, a mentor, a medicine chest with healing for what ails me."

With deep feeling Ralph tells the story of how he bared his soul to his church family. It was the hardest sermon he had ever preached. He called it an emotional Everest. But when it was over, people hugged him and shared with him their own deep awareness of what Ralph had experienced. "That's me, too." "You were telling my story." "Please pray for me," many people said. Now Ralph admits, as he speaks about his church, "I've seen the miracle of God's domino effect. He uses the vulnerability, the brokenness, and subsequent healing of one person to set the tone for others. His Spirit is softening stony hearts, pretense is being discarded, and the peace that passes all understanding gives evidence of renewal." With tears of joy in his eyes he explains, "Thanks be to God who through Jesus Christ our Lord releases us from the prison of an empty Christian shell." Here are facts, faith, and feelings in beautiful balance.

Conscious of His Coming

Cohesive Contrasts

After a group has been together for a few weeks it sometimes moves from the "honeymoon" to "disillusionment" stage. This is the most important time for the group to really persist in nuturing each other and reaching out to the community to invite others in. Here is a "getting to understand you" question.

Have you ever felt a deep thirst for something that seemed lacking? For example, water, understanding, love. How was that thirst quenched?

Consideration of the Word
Study Text: Luke 11:1-13

What feelings take place when the man in Jesus' story receives all he needs (Luke 11:8)?

"It's about time" _____ "Why did He make me wait?" _____

Deep gratitude _____ "Praise the Lord" _____

Relief _____ Joy _____ Other _____

What made you aware from reading chapter five that God has whole "loaves" of the Holy Spirit for us when we have been experiencing just a few "crumbs"?

_____

_____

_____

If we are to be filled with the Holy Spirit, we must have a deep longing for this to happen. Why, do you think, would God especially illustrate this with thirst for water (Psalm 42:1, 2)? _____

_____

_____

In Luke 11 Jesus connects prayer to the persistence that results in abundance of bread. What type of prayer do you see illustrated here? For example, earnest, routine, rapid, etc. _____

_____

_____

In contrast to the individual prayer of the man needing bread, Acts pictures the power of group prayer. Notice Acts 1:14; 4:24-31. How has the earnestness of the prayers of others in your small group influenced you? _____

_____

_____

The transition between asking and receiving is based not on feeling but faith (Galatians 3:14). List some ways Jesus inspires us in Luke 11:9-13 to take the step of faith. _____

_____

_____

Describe "faith" in your own words. _____

_____

_____

If I have been "asking, seeking, knocking" for the Holy Spirit in deep earnestness and have by faith trusted that God has answered, what feelings may I now have?

Love _____ Hope _____ Praise_____

Songs in my heart _____ Peace _____ Joy_____

Quietness _____ Assurance _____ Confidence _____

Others _____

When should we repress happy feelings and when should we express them?

_____

_____

_____

Why is it a relief to know that your salvation and filling with the Spirit is not based on feelings but on faith that comes from Jesus? _____

_____

_____

Conversation With the Lord

First, by faith thank God for hearing a specific prayer that you have prayed. It may even be for something you have not yet seen a visible answer to.

Second, ask God for a deep thirsting and longing for the Spirit and righteousness of God. Pray that each member of your group will be really thirsty.

Third, pray for specific needs of group members and their families. Minister to each other.

Conclude with the Lord's Prayer.

Committing the Word to Memory

This week, write out Luke 11:13. Memorize this verse, then share it with someone as soon as possible.

_____

_____

_____

_____

"Surrender" Is a Victory Word

I have prayed many times for the Holy Spirit, but I don't seem to get an answer." "At church I always ask God to send His Spirit, but nothing seems to change." "Some people just bubble over with the Spirit, but everything in my life seems flat and uneventful."

I have heard statements like these many times. You may have heard them too, even from your own lips. "Read my lips," you say. "No new spirit, just the same old routine."

Each of the above statements contains two words that are indicative of a problem. One is "but," and the other is "seems." These words tell of individual experiences in which people look at themselves and others and cannot balance what they see with how they feel.

Perhaps if this has been your experience, you have looked for wrong evidences of the Holy Spirit. A number of sections in this book will help you know the true signs of receiving the filling of the Holy Spirit, but at this time we want to consider the possibility that there is a blockage hindering the flow of the Holy Spirit. Listen. That blockage can be eliminated right now by the power of the Holy Spirit, and the result will be absolutely amazing.

Notice what is said about Jesus in Hebrews 1:9: "You have loved righteousness and hated lawlessness; therefore God, Your God, has anointed You with the oil of gladness more than Your companions." William W. Prescott, who was at one time simultaneously president of three colleges and was known as an exceptional Bible teacher, spoke at length on Hebrews 1:9 during a series of sermons on the Holy Spirit. He explained that the word "companions," or "followers," is translated "partners" in Luke 5:7.[1] Why did Jesus have more of the oil of gladness than His partners? That is the question we ask as we also wonder about ourselves. Why do others seem to have a more vibrant Christian experience than I do?

The New Testament word "gladness" in Hebrews 1:9 is interesting. It means exceedingly joyful or leaping for joy. Even before Jesus was born He brought gladness to another in a remarkable way. Read the story in Luke 1:34-44. When Mary the mother of Jesus was a few months' pregnant, she journeyed to visit her cousin Elizabeth who was pregnant with John the Baptist. When Elizabeth heard the greeting of Mary, "the babe leaped in her womb" (verse 41). Jesus apparently even had a prenatal ministry of gladness.

But when Jesus was formally anointed for His public ministry, the oil of gladness was revealed as never before. "How God anointed Jesus of Nazareth with the Holy Spirit and with power, who went about doing good and healing all who were oppressed by the devil, for God was with Him" (Acts 10:38). Jesus went about doing good and healing, and the result was unprecedented gladness for many. The ministry of Jesus always brings gladness in the midst of all the problems and pressures of life.

At a large General Conference convention of my church I was greeted enthusiastically by a young minister whom I had not seen for some time. "Remember me?" Tim said. "Remember how I suffered terrible back pain? When we last met, I was in real agony most of the time." Yes, I remembered Tim. I had come to know him at a pastor's Holy Spirit Fellowship. He had shared some of his frustrations in ministry and the story of long and painful back problems. Tim had asked for prayer and anointing and afterward said his back felt easier. Now six months later he was full of gladness and almost leaping for joy. "X-rays have confirmed that my back has been miraculously healed."

Just before I met Tim again, Dr. Adrian Peterson introduced me to an elderly lady who, although rather frail, was beaming for joy. "This is one of our miracle ladies," the pastor explained. One winter day Cornelia Lay had felt strongly impressed to call the Indiana Adventist Book Center and order a book to be sent to her home. She did not know why she wanted the book at that time, but believed that the Lord was strongly impressing her to take this action. Then she stated that the book must be delivered by the United Parcel Service. Cornelia lived in a small country home with no close neighbors. A few days after ordering the book, she walked out of her house about 10:30 a.m. and without a moment's warning slipped and fell into the snow, injuring her shoulder on some hard object on the ground below. All day Cornelia remained in the snow, unable to lift herself or move back to the house. As darkness began to creep across the frozen landscape like an omen of certain death, the miracle took place.

The United Parcel Service delivery agent arrived with Cornelia's book and, finding this elderly injured lady in the snow, was able to save her life. Today Mrs. Lay is filled with the oil of gladness as she tells her story.

Jesus in His ministry saved many lives physically and spiritually. Obviously He did not have the spirit by measure (John 3:34). The oil of gladness filled His life in spite of the fact that He was a man of sorrows and acquainted with grief. The secret of His greatness is seen in Hebrews 1:9: He "loved righteousness and hated lawlessness." That may sound sweet and easy, but you know as well as I do that to love righteousness and hate sin is about as natural to the unconverted heart as flying is to sheep. Jesus is an incredible example of what is possible to any person by total surrender to God. His ministry began and ended this way. "For I have come down from heaven, not to do My own will, but the will of Him that sent Me" (John 6:38). "O My Father, if it is possible, let this cup pass from Me; nevertheless, not as I will, but as You will" (Matthew 26:39).

There is absolutely no barrier to the outpouring of the Holy Spirit that cannot be evaporated by complete surrender to God. In fact, I believe that the filling of a person's life with the Holy Spirit is actually another way of describing a life totally surrendered to God.

Are you concerned that your life has not had the spiritual power that you vaguely or earnestly desire? Perhaps some of the barriers to absolute surrender have barred the way like a military roadblock in the modern Middle East. I have come upon them a number of times on the road from Jericho to Amman. A single lane of road between large concrete blocks is covered with a mat of viscious spikes. Soldiers with submachine guns block the way. Tanks line the side of the road. Onward progress is extremely unlikely. In a *Desire of Ages* chapter that mentions the Holy Spirit about 30 times on two pages is this statement: "Christ has promised the gift of the Holy Spirit to His church, and the promise belongs to us as much as to the first disciples. But like every other promise, it is given on conditions. There are many who believe and profess to claim the Lord's promise; they talk *about* Christ and *about* the Holy Spirit, yet receive no benefit. They do not surrender the soul to be guided and controlled by the divine agencies. We cannot use the Holy Spirit. The Spirit is to use us. Through the Spirit God works in His people 'to will and to do of his good pleasure' (Philippians 2:13, KJV). But many will not submit to this. They want to manage themselves. This is why they do not receive the heavenly gift." [2]

Think with me through the four major barriers to total surrender and the complete filling of our life with the Holy Spirit.

Deceived by Deliberate Sin

The thought of deliberate sin makes most of us stop in our tracks. "I would never deliberately sin," we say. "I only slipped accidentally, unintentionally into sin." Look with me at this verse in Psalm 66: "If I regard iniquity in my heart, the Lord will not hear" (verse 18). The New International Version talks about cherishing sin in the heart. This means approving, secretly enjoying, secretly experiencing. A lot of television feeds this sort of mental attitude, in which sin is enjoyed and experienced in the mind secondhand. Jesus hated sin. Therefore, He was anointed with the oil of gladness more than His companions.

It may be painful, but it is necessary to examine ourselves regularly. For instance, take the Ten Commandments (printed on the opposite page) and pray through them one by one, asking if there is one or more of these you are actually disregarding, ignoring, breaking outwardly or in the mind. This is a little scary, but the Holy Spirit will begin to convince you of sin. He will do it gently and gradually, but as it happens, ask Him for complete victory power. Although you may continue to be tempted by a certain sin, you will hate it and will turn from it constantly.

Read carefully through the whole New Testament. It will take only about 12 hours. You could do that in 12 days or over one weekend. Ask that God will reveal to you what He wants you to know at this time. Every time I do this, God convicts me of new sins to deal with by His strength in my life. Pray the psalmist's prayer, "Search me, O God, and know my heart; try me, and know my anxieties; and see if there is any wicked way in me, and lead me in the way everlasting" (Psalm 139:23, 24).

I used to think that the Holy Spirit was given only to those who perfectly obey. After all, Acts 5:32 does say, "The Holy Spirit whom God has given to those who obey Him." Pastor Kevin Wilfley helped me understand this more clearly when he said, "The Greek word here translated 'obey' is *peitharcheo,* which literally means to be persuaded by a ruler or to submit to authority. It comes from the word *peitho,* which means to agree, believe, have confidence, make friends. And the word *archo,* which means to reign or rule over. Therefore, the Holy Spirit is given to them who make friends with God, who submit to His authority or rule over their lives." [3]

I receive the fullness of the Holy Spirit each day not by perfectly obeying but by being willing to obey. If I am not willing, then I need to

I

Thou shalt have no other gods before Me.

II

Thou shalt not make unto thee any graven image, or any likeness of anything that is in heaven above, or that is in the earth beneath, or that is in the water under the earth: thou shalt not bow down thyself to them, nor serve them: for I the Lord thy God am a jealous God, visiting the iniquity of the fathers upon the children unto the third and fourth generation of them that hate Me; and showing mercy unto thousands of them that love Me, and keep My commandments.

III

Thou shalt not take the name of the Lord thy God in vain; for the Lord will not hold him guiltless that taketh His name in vain.

IV

Remember the Sabbath day, to keep it holy. Six days shalt thou labor, and do all thy work: but the seventh day is the Sabbath of the Lord thy God: in it thou shalt not do any work, thou, nor thy son, nor thy daughter, thy manservant, nor thy maidservant, nor thy cattle, nor thy stranger that is within thy gates: for in six days the Lord made heaven and earth, the sea, and all that in them is, and rested the seventh day: wherefore the Lord blessed the Sabbath day, and hallowed it.

V

Honor thy father and thy mother: that thy days may be long upon the land which the Lord thy God giveth thee.

VI

Thou shalt not kill.

VII

Thou shalt not commit adultery.

VIII

Thou shalt not steal.

IX

Thou shalt not bear false witness against thy neighbor.

X

Thou shalt not covet thy neighbor's house, thou shalt not covet thy neighbor's wife, nor his manservant, nor his maidservant, nor his ox, nor his ass, nor anything that is thy neighbor's.

pray, "O Lord, please help me to be willing to be made willing."

As we pray through the Ten Commandments and the New Testament (or the whole Bible, for that matter), the Holy Spirit will lead us into all truth. The conflicts between right and wrong within us may be intense, but God is almighty. God will see us through.

I listened to Dr. Ben Carson, the famous neurosurgeon, tell of his struggle with sin when he was a 14-year-old Black youth in a Boston ghetto. In a moment of terrible anger he had almost stabbed a friend. Fortunately, his knife blade had been broken by his friend's belt buckle. Ben realized that his temper was uncontrollable, so he raced home and locked himself in the bathroom and there struggled for hours with his temper and with God. "Unless I get rid of this temper," Ben said, "I'm not going to make it. If Bob hadn't worn that big buckle he'd probably be dead, and I'd be on my way to jail or reform school." Ben tells how misery rushed over him. Sweat trickled down his armpits and his sides. He hated himself, but he felt that because of his temper he couldn't help himself. Then from somewhere deep inside came the impression to pray, and he prayed as he never had before. He prayed knowing from his reading of *Psychology Today* that it is considered impossible to change the personality trait of a bad temper. With tears streaming down he prayed, "Lord, despite all what the experts tell me, You can change me. You can free me forever from this destructive personality trait." Hours of misery engulfed him in darkness, but in the midst of this he began to read the Bible as he prayed. In Proverbs he read, "He who is slow to anger is better than the mighty, and he who rules his spirit than he who takes a city" (Proverbs 16:32, RSV). Then Ben tells the amazing climax of those hours of terrible struggle with sin. "After a while peace began to fill my mind. My hands quit shaking. The tears stopped. During those hours alone in the bathroom, something happened to me. God heard my deep cries of anguish. A feeling of lightness flowed over me, and I knew a change of heart had taken place. I felt different. I was different. At last I stood up, placed the Bible on the edge of the tub, and went to the sink. I washed my face and hands, and straightened my clothes. I walked out of the bathroom a changed young man. 'My temper will never control me again,' I told myself. 'Never again. I'm free.' And since that day, since those long hours wrestling with myself and crying to God for help, I have never had a problem with my temper."[4]

Wrecked by Wrong Motives

Motive is a hidden desire or reason behind a certain action. Motive is not always clear on the surface. A company offers you a free trip to a beautiful luxury resort. You say, "Hold on, what is their motive?" You offer to dig a neighbor's garden. She says, "Why are you doing this for me?"

When I ask for the Holy Spirit, what is my motive? Does God care? Apparently. "You ask and do not receive, because you ask amiss, that you may spend it on your pleasures" (James 4:3).

In ancient Samaria there was an influential man, Simon, who was baptized into Christianity, but apparently still had wrong motives. He surprised Peter and John by offering them money for the power of the Holy Spirit. Notice how strongly Peter dealt with the situation. Peter said to him, "Your money perish with you, because you thought that the gift of God could be purchased with money!" Obviously, a gift cannot and need not be purchased. Here is evidence of an unconverted heart. "You have neither part nor portion in this matter, for your heart is not right in the sight of God." Now Peter lays his finger on the heart of the problem. "For I see you are poisoned by bitterness and bound by iniquity" (Acts 8:20-23). How often bitterness poisons a life and iniquity binds the mind and heart like a steel chain. Many times we miss out on the full blessing of the Holy Spirit because bitterness and iniquity tarnish our motives.

Often the five P's—position, power, prestige, popularity, and profit—dominate our lives. Jesus turned away from all these and in so doing was anointed with the oil of gladness above His companions.

I was pastoring a small church in Sydney years ago when a man came to me with the tearful plea that I would pray for him to receive the Holy Spirit. I am not sure what denomination he claimed, but when I asked him why he wanted the Holy Spirit so desperately, he indicated that the motive was peer pressure. "This is your only way to be as good as us," his friends had implied. I asked Bill to examine his motives, and when he refused, I could only pray that the Holy Spirit would lead him to the cross. There motives are molded by the love of Jesus.

Stumbling Over Self-centeredness

A selfish pride is so foolish in comparison to heaven. Recently some of those little mounds of dirt we call molehills began to appear on our lovely green lawn. Those moles had a great time turning our backyard into a miniature of the Canadian Rockies. Perhaps there was a proud mole who considered his molehill higher than all the others. G. B. Thompson writing on the Holy Spirit quotes the great Scottish preacher Alexander Maclaren. "Granted that you are superior to me in something or other. Well, what does that matter? One molehill is a little higher than another, but they are all about the same distance from the sun. I remember a friend of mine who, when a child, being told that the sun was 95 million miles off, asked whether it was from the upstairs window or the downstairs." [5]

The rich and poor, educated and uneducated, handsome and plain, are all about the same distance from heaven without Jesus Christ. Human self-centeredness is pitiful and pathetic because it is totally futile in the end.

Notice how truly humble Jesus really was. "Let this mind be in you which was also in Christ Jesus, who, being in the form of God, did not consider it robbery to be equal with God, but made Himself of no reputation, taking the form of a servant, and coming in the likeness of men. And being found in the appearance as a man, He humbled Himself and became obedient to the point of death, even the death of the cross" (Philippians 2:5-8).

That beautiful commentary on the life of Jesus, *The Desire of Ages,* contrasts self-centeredness with the true spirit of Jesus. "His own disciples were so filled with self-seeking—the very principle of Satan's kingdom." [6] "We can receive of heaven's light only as we are willing to be emptied of self." [7] Perhaps the statement that impressed me most as an 18-year-old was this: "There is no limit to the usefulness of one who, by putting self aside, makes room for the working of the Holy Spirit upon his heart, and lives a life wholly consecrated to God." [8]

Yes, "surrender" is a victory word. As I open my life in total surrender to God, the limitless power of the Holy Spirit enables me to really live for God in gladness and true success.

Undermined by Unbelief

Deliberate sin, wrong motives, and self-centeredness are a formidable array of barriers that stand between many Christians and the true power of the Holy Spirit. This unholy trio have their roots in a much more basic problem, namely, lack of total belief in Jesus. I do not mean intellectual belief, but a daily heart surrender to the Lordship of Jesus.

Often longstanding church members would be offended if I as a pastor confronted them with the bold assertion "I am going to teach you how to receive Jesus into your life as a personal Saviour." Many times, however, when I was conducting classes to teach church members how to lead others to Jesus, these pillars of the church would explain, "I did not understand this myself. What you say is so simple and clear to me." "Let us kneel down and open our hearts to Jesus right now," I would respond. The results were always amazing. What gladness to hear a church elder stand up and say, with tears in his eyes, "I know for the first time what it means to be born again."

Here lies the root of our problem. Many are cultural Christians but have never come to really know Jesus as Saviour, Lord, and Friend. Look at the way Jesus combined "belief" and "Holy Spirit" when He spoke at the Jerusalem Temple. "On the last day, that great day of the feast, Jesus stood and cried out, saying, 'If anyone thirsts, let him come to Me and drink. He who believes in Me, as the Scripture has said, out of his heart will flow rivers of living water.' But this He spoke concerning the Spirit, whom those believing in Him would receive; for the Holy Spirit was not yet given, because Jesus was not yet glorified" (John 7:37-39).

An enthusiastic theology student joined his professor who had led Bible studies in a local prison for 14 years. The group began to explore the *Window to John's Gospel* study guides,[9] and the beautiful combination of the ministry of Jesus with the power of the Holy Spirit began to bring evidences of conversion in the lives of inmates who attended. Prison walls are no barrier to the Holy Spirit; neither is there any barrier within us that cannot be overcome by surrender to the love of Jesus.

Remember from our earlier studies that it is at conversion that the Holy Spirit enters the life. He cannot fill a life that He has not already regenerated. If you are sensing any barrier at all to the Holy Spirit, I simply ask you to open your heart fully to Jesus right now. You will not be disappointed. Remember, "surrender" is a victory word.

"Surrender" Is a Victory Word

Cohesive Contrasts

Inner cohesiveness or bonding is often revealed in a group by such external clues as body language, tone of voice, facial expressions, and levels of attention. By now you will have seen the value of some "give and take" with a lot of acceptance and forgiveness. Look out for signals of some "surrender" of self-centeredness, and praise all the indications of growing togetherness in your group.

Here is an interesting interaction exercise. Take a piece of paper and draw three boxes. Using two stick figures or one word in each box, illustrate how you first perceived the group, and how you see it now. In the third box, identify your cohesive goal for the group. Compare similarities and differences in the boxes of each group member.

Consideration of the Word
Study Text: Acts 8:12-25

What word immediately comes to mind when you think of surrender?
_____

My surrender to God is an indication of

Failure _____ Defeat _____ My weakness _____

God's opposition to me _____ My openness to God's leading _____

Other _____

What connection do you see between Jesus' complete filling with the Spirit and

His total surrender to the will of the Father (John 6:38; Matthew 26:39)? ___

_____

Because sin is so deceptive, how easy is it to examine ourselves honestly to see if there is a deliberate disregard of God's Word that is blocking the way to complete surrender to God? _____

_____

How will the psalmist's prayer help us (Psalm 139:23, 24)? _____

_____

What caused the baptized believer Simon to be disqualified from receiving the filling of the Holy Spirit? List at least four reasons from Acts 8:18-23. _____

_____

Have you ever known someone "poisoned by bitterness"? How was that person's whole life gradually affected by this? _____

_____

Jesus' rejection of self-centeredness is seen in Philippians 2:5-8. Like Jesus, Peter, Philip, and John were filled with the Holy Spirit. How do their characters stand in contrast to that of Simon (Acts 8:13-23)? _____

_____

How can the Holy Spirit help us put self aside without us losing our realization of self-worth in Jesus? _____

_____

Total belief in Jesus is the essence of complete surrender to the will of God. Why do you think this attitude makes it possible for a person to be anointed with the "oil of gladness" (Hebrews 1:9)? _____

_____

Of the four barriers to complete surrender and filling with the Holy Spirit studied in this chapter, which do you see as the most deceptive and dangerous in Christian churches today? Why? _____

_____

What one thing above all else leads you to surrender fully to God today? ____

_____

Conversation With the Lord

Perhaps there are some beautiful prayer songs of surrender your group may want to sing together. If some in the group are unfamiliar with these songs, those who know the words and tunes may sing them a number of times so all can learn them.

First, share prayers of praise.

Second, ask that God's will be done in the life of each group member. Put any barriers into the hands of God, to be broken down by the power of the Holy Spirit.

Third, pray for specific needs.

Conclude as usual with the Lord's Prayer.

Committing the Word to Memory

This week, write out Acts 8:17-19. Memorize these verses, then share them with someone as soon as possible.

_____

_____

CHAPTER
SEVEN
▼

Inner Witness
or Imagination?

After a Holy Spirit Fellowship retreat a pastor drove home with the words of the theme song ringing in his ears. Over and over during the next week part of one line was repeated in his mind. "I know who I am." When the Spirit fills my heart and mind, as the song says, I will know who I am and because of that will want to throw my arms around my wonderful God, exclaiming, "Abba, Father." *Abba* was a special word for Father in the language the Jewish people used in Palestine during the lifetime of Jesus. Only children of the family could speak this way. A servant could not use this word. It was used especially by little children as, in a loving and very intimate way, they addressed their father. When Jesus said "Abba, Father" in the Garden of Gethsemane (Mark 14:36), it indicated a closeness to God beyond anything the rabbis understood.

Spirit-filled Christians also experience that special Abba closeness to their heavenly Father. In the greatest Holy Spirit chapter in the Bible Paul says that through the Spirit of adoption we cry out, not in fear but in love, "Abba, Father" (Romans 8:15). Notice how this is connected to the Holy Spirit and the heavenly family in Galatians. "And because you are sons, God has sent forth the Spirit of His Son into your hearts, crying out, 'Abba, Father!'" (Galatians 4:6). When through the Holy Spirit you really know who you are, you will come to God each day in prayer and with the simplicity of childlike faith say, "Abba, Father."

Abba is a little bit like the English word "Daddy." When our own daughters were small, they all called me Daddy. Eventually they grew out of it except on special occasions. When our middle daughter, Lyndell, was about 18 years old, she decided she needed her driver's license. Barbara and I were to leave for a seminar in two weeks when Lyndell announced that she would have her license before we flew to Florida. Now, I knew that Lyndell is very determined and of an independent spirit, but still I stomped around the house exclaiming decisively that it would

75

The Spirit Bears Witness

Garrie F. Williams

Corleen Johnson

be impossible to learn to drive and get a license in two weeks. I suppose my actions provided even more incentive, because sure enough, with a few days to spare she came home with that important piece of plastic that enabled her to take the family car out onto the road. After that, Lyndell on occasions would sweetly call me Daddy, which I knew was a signal she wanted the car keys.

Without conversion it is possible to work on Christianity learning how to benefit from the many advantages of church membership. We can be licensed to hold church office, but it is only as the Holy Spirit opens our mind to the love of God and we come to God from no ulterior motive that we can have a real "Abba" relationship with our heavenly Father.

A Word From the Inner Witness

Let us study together the importance of the "inner witness" of the Spirit. This is the secret of the tremendous certainty and assurance God's spirit-filled people have. Incidentally, following the "Abba" verse in Romans 8, Paul says, "The Spirit Himself bears witness with our spirit that we are children of God" (verse 16). It is the witness of the Spirit that enables Christians to know who they are.

"Who are you? Are you a child of God?" Some Christians reply, "I hope so." "I'm not quite sure." "I believe I am a child of God, but I don't like admitting it publicly as it may sound egotistical." I listened to a radio interview with the son of former U.S. president Ronald Reagan. Ron Reagan, Jr., was asked, "What is it like to be the son of a president?" Imagine the listeners' surprise if he had answered, "I'm not quite sure who I am, really. Even if Ronald Reagan is my father, I am hesitant to admit it."

Jesus made it possible for those who believe in Him to be the children of God. "But as many as received Him, to them He gave the right to become children of God, even to those who believed in His name" (John 1:12). Notice the certainty that Jesus' New Testament followers expressed: "You are no longer a slave but a son" (Galatians 4:7). "Now we *are* the children of God" (1 John 3:2). Because of this certainty it has been said, "You will ever find with the true Christian a marked cheerfulness, a holy, happy confidence in God, a submission to His providences, that is refreshing to the soul." [1]

Steps to Christ, which has led millions to a certainty of faith and acceptance in Jesus Christ, contains this passage: "Do not wait to *feel* that you are made whole, but say, 'I believe it; it *is* so, not because I feel it, but because God has promised.' Jesus says, 'What things soever ye desire, when ye pray, believe that ye receive them, and ye shall have them' (Mark 11:24, KJV). There is a condition to this promise—that we pray according to the will of God. But it is the will of God to cleanse us from sin, to make us His children, and to enable us to live a holy life. So we may ask of these blessings, and believe that we receive them, and thank God that we *have* received them. . . . Through this simple act of believing God, the Holy Spirit has begotten a new life in your heart. You are as a child born into the family of God, and He loves you as He loves His Son." [2]

When John Wesley was sailing to America, his ship encountered a severe storm, and it seemed as though all would be lost. The terrible screaming among the English passengers in contrast to the peace and sweet songs of the German Moravian Christians led John Wesley after reaching America to ask Moravian Bishop Spangenberg for spiritual counsel. Here is the heart of the interview as recorded by Wesley himself on February 7, 1736. Spangenberg said, " 'My brother, I must first ask you one or two questions. Have you the witness within yourself? Does the Spirit of God bear witness with your spirit, that you are a child of God?' I was surprised, and I knew not what to answer. He observed it, and asked, 'Do you know Jesus Christ?' I paused, and said, 'I know He is the Saviour of the world.' 'True,' replied he; 'but do you know He has saved you?' I answered, 'I hope He has died to save me.' He only added, 'Do you know yourself?' I said, 'I do.' But I fear they were vain words."

How would you answer if you were asked the same question? Does the Spirit bear witness with your spirit that you are a child of God? It was at the New Year's Eve prayer meeting in Fetter Lane that the witness of the Spirit came to John Wesley on January 1, 1739, at 3:00 a.m., as we noticed in chapter five.

John Wesley and the early Methodists also spoke of the "inner witness" of the Spirit. This they found in the study of the first letter of John. "This is He who came by water and blood—Jesus Christ; not only by water, but by water and blood. And it is the Spirit who bears witness, because the Spirit is truth" (1 John 5:6). Now where is it that the Holy Spirit bears witness? Notice verse 10: "He who believes in the Son of God has the witness in himself." So again I ask, "Do you have the inner witness of the Spirit? Do you have the witness in yourself?"

Is it possible to really know the inner witness, or must we be content with a shaky faith? In the New Testament it was expected that people would know whether or not they had received the Holy Spirit. Notice what happened when Paul came to Ephesus. He asked the disciples, "Did you receive the Holy Spirit when you believed?" (Acts 19:2). One thing is certain. Paul expected these people and all Christians to know whether or not they had received the Holy Spirit. When seven deacons were to be chosen, the qualifications for this church office were to be obvious. "Therefore, brethren, seek out from among you seven men of good reputation, full of the Holy Spirit and wisdom, whom we may appoint over this business" (Acts 6:3).

You can know today and every day whether or not you are filled with the Spirit. There is no need to be painfully indefinite. You do not have to walk in uncertainty. "For our gospel did not come to you in word only, but also in power, and in the Holy Spirit and in much assurance, as you know what kind of men we were among you for your sake" (1 Thessalonians 1:5). "The work of righteousness will be peace, and the effect of righteousness, quietness and assurance forever" (Isaiah 32:17).

I have often noticed this certainty in the writings of the pioneers in my denomination. James White describes his experiences at the home of John Loughborough in Santa Rosa, California. "At one time, while we were knelt in prayer, and Mrs. White took my arm and bade me rise and go free, as I arose, the Holy Ghost came upon us in such a measure that we both fell to the floor. I now feel sure that God has forgiven my sins, so far as I have seen them, and confessed them in the spirit of true repentance. My sins do not longer separate me from God. And as I have made a determined effort to draw nigh to God, He has come very nigh to me. That terrible weight of discouragement and gloom that has been upon me much of the time for the past two years is gone from me, and hope, courage, peace, and joy have taken its place."[3] This experience, which was very similar to that of John Wesley, brought assurance of forgiven sins, and the resulting feelings were positive and full of joy. Later James's wife, Ellen, wrote, "The Holy Spirit is a person, for He beareth witness with our spirits that we are the children of God. When this witness is borne, it carries with it its own evidence. At such times we believe and are sure that we are the children of God."[4] The witness of the Spirit carries "its own evidence," helping a person to be "sure" that he or she is a child of God.

Follow me as I go step by step through the journey to assurance. It is a familiar path because, like many other Christians, I walk this road each day.

Sure About Blessed Assurance

First, let us review our study in chapter five. As we come into the Lord's presence each day, opening our heart in sincerity to God, there is created within us by the Holy Spirit a great thirst and a deep longing for righteousness and the inner strength of Jesus (Matthew 5:6; John 7:37-39). Sometimes it may take hours or even days of prayer and feeding upon the Word before this hunger and thirst are fully realized. If we are walking close to God, this deep longing will come almost spontaneously each day and sometimes many times during the day. In the midst of this longing comes the time to take the step of faith, believing that God has fulfilled His promise and heard and answered the prayer.

It is as the fruitage of faith that the Spirit's witness comes. It does not replace faith as the basis of salvation, but does bring a new dimension to the daily Christian experience. This is where fact and faith come to fruition in feeling. Paul expressed this beautifully in his prayer to the Ephesians: "That he would grant you, according to the riches of His glory, to be strengthened with might through His Spirit in the inner man, that Christ may dwell in your hearts through faith; and that you, being rooted and grounded in love, may be able to comprehend with all the saints what is the width and length and depth and height—to know the love of Christ which passes knowledge; that you may be filled with all the fullness of God" (Ephesians 3:16-19). I often ask people to claim the promise of Ephesians 3:16 for me, that I will be "strengthened with might through His Spirit in the inner man."

Let me walk with you through some statements that have really helped me here. Talking of fervent prayer, we read, "Do not leave your closet until you feel strong in God . . ."[5] A few pages later in the same book: "Do not neglect secret prayer, for it is the soul of religion. With earnest, fervent prayer, plead for purity of soul. Plead as earnestly, as eagerly, as you would for your mortal life, were it at stake. Remain before God until unutterable longings are begotten within you for salvation, and the sweet evidence is obtained of pardoned sin."[6]

Here is the balance between the "deep longings" and the "sweet evidence." Earlier we noticed that the witness of the Spirit carries "its own evidence," bringing sureness and certainty. All of this feeling that is the fruitage of faith is the blessing God wants His people to enjoy.

Let me emphasize again, your salvation and filling with the Spirit is not the result of feeling, nor does it depend on feeling. Certainly not. When you believe in Jesus, accept Him as your Saviour, and claim by faith that

He has fulfilled His promise to give you the Holy Spirit, then it is so, no matter how you feel (Ephesians 2:8, 9; Galatians 3:14). But God has apparently not designed Christianity to be a feelingless religion stoically believed by people who are not moved in heart and spirit by anything other than the mundane matters of life. "And the disciples were filled with joy and with the Holy Spirit" (Acts 13:52). "Now may the God of hope fill you with all joy and peace in believing that you may abound in hope by the power of the Holy Spirit" (Romans 15:13). "And you became followers of us and of the Lord, having received the word in much affliction, with joy of the Holy Spirit" (1 Thessalonians 1:6).

Recently I found a statement that helped me understand the delicate balance between faith and the feeling of blessings from God. "Feeling is not faith; the two are distinct. Faith is ours to exercise, but joyful feeling and the blessing are God's to give. . . . Here is faith, naked faith, to believe that we receive the blessing, even before we realize it. When the promised blessing is realized and enjoyed, faith is swallowed up. But many suppose they have much faith when sharing largely of the Holy Spirit, and that they cannot have faith unless they feel the power of the Spirit. Such confound faith with the blessing that comes through faith. The very time to exercise faith is when we feel destitute of the Spirit." [7] When the promised blessing comes, there is such joy, calm assurance, and certainty that, as the author says, faith is swallowed up. The sweet evidence of pardoned sins and integration into the family of God is so great that faith is superseded by tears of joy, magnetic hopefulness, and victory power.

John Wesley records in his journal the certainty that came to his godly mother, Susanna. "Monday, September 3. I talked largely with my mother, who told me that, till a short time since, she had scarce heard such a thing mentioned as the having forgiveness of sins now, or God's Spirit bearing witness with our spirit: much less did she imagine that this was the common privilege of all true believers. 'Therefore,' said she, 'I never durst ask it for myself. But two or three weeks ago, while my son Hall was pronouncing those words in delivering the cup to me, "The blood of our Lord Jesus Christ, which was given for thee," the words struck through my heart, and I knew God for Christ's sake had forgiven *me* all *my* sins.' " John's brother, Charles, wrote thousands of hymns that expressed this same conviction. "O for a thousand tongues to sing my great Redeemer's praise!" Fanny Crosby wrote, "Blessed assurance, Jesus is mine!" and "Redeemed! how I love to proclaim it! . . . His child, and forever, I am."

Hattie Buel wrote, "I'm a child of the King, a child of the King! With Jesus, my Saviour, I'm a child of the King!"

I have often heard evidence of this inner conviction as I have listened to Kevin Wilfley sharing his experience with the Lord. "I cannot personally point to an exact time and say when I received the baptism of the Holy Spirit, although I remember the day and the occasion I first knew I had the conviction of His presence. My heart welled up in praise and tears came to my eyes as I realized the blessing I had been so consistently asking for had been bestowed. Much like the wind that Jesus compared the Holy Spirit to I do not recall exactly when the wind began to blow, but of its blowing I now am sure. . . . What a change has taken place in my life. I want to praise God like I never did before. I have a contentment in my heart. I seem to be more at peace with my fellow church members, my wife, my children, and others. I have assurance of salvation and power to overcome sins. My prayer life has changed, and my understanding of and appreciation for the Bible has increased. My ministry is more effective, and I am more satisfied in the position I find myself in. In short, I am a new creature in Christ Jesus." [8]

Examining Human Excitement

The excitement, joy, and spiritual blessing that comes from the inner witness of the Spirit, however, necessitates us looking at all of this now from another perspective. Rather than seeing the emotional elevation as a fruitage of faith, some have seen this as the foundation. When this happens, emotionalism and human excitement begin to dominate, and these are often manufactured artificially. Some types of music are used to build up an emotional high. People are worked into a frenzy in a religious gathering, and finally they reach a high point that is signaled by various body contortions and nonsensical sounds. These are held up as God's signs of blessing, and the people are led to believe that they have now received the Holy Spirit. The desire for submission to Jesus and the willingness to follow and obey His Word is now pushed aside in favor of a human excitement.

Some forms of Christianity have fallen into this trap. George Canty, former president of the Elim Pentecostal Church (Worldwide), records a prophecy that was made in 1906 at the beginning of the Pentecostal movements at Azusa Street in Los Angeles. "In the last days just before the return of Jesus Christ: 1. In Pentecostal circles there will be an overemphasis on power rather than righteousness. 2. There will be an emphasis on praise to a God they no longer pray to. 3. There will be an emphasis on gifts rather than the Lordship of Jesus Christ." [9]

Even in my own denomination there have been times when artificial emotionalism has arisen. Back in 1900 an observer of events in Indiana wrote, "The manner in which the meetings in Indiana have been carried on, with noise and confusion, does not commend them to thoughtful, intelligent minds. There is nothing in these demonstrations which will convince the world that we have the truth. Mere noise and shouting are no evidence of sanctification, or of the descent of the Holy Spirit. . . . The things that you have described as taking place in Indiana, the Lord has shown me would take place just before the close of probation. Every uncouth thing will be demonstrated. There will be shouting, with drums, music, and dancing. The senses of rational beings will become so confused that they cannot be trusted to make right decisions. And this is called the moving of the Holy Spirit. . . . A bedlam of noise shocks the senses and perverts that which if conducted aright might be a blessing. The power of satanic agencies blend with the din and noise, to have a carnival, and this is termed the Holy Spirit's working." [10]

But does all this mean that the true fruitage of the inner witness of the Spirit must be avoided? No, not according to the writers of the Bible. When the disciples of Jesus "began to rejoice and praise God with a loud voice," the Pharisees asked Jesus to rebuke His disciples. He replied, "I tell you that if these should keep silent, the stones would immediately cry out" (Luke 19:37-40). After Jesus' ascension the disciples "worshiped Him, and returned to Jerusalem with great joy, and were continually in the temple praising and blessing God" (Luke 24:52, 53). The writer of Hebrews emphasized, "Therefore by Him let us continually offer the sacrifice of praise to God, that is, the fruit of our lips, giving thanks to His name" (Hebrews 13:15). Peter also was convicted of the necessity of openly praising God. "Though now you do not see Him, yet believing, you rejoice with joy inexpressible and full of glory" (1 Peter 1:8). "You are a chosen generation, a royal priesthood, a holy nation, His own special people, that you may proclaim the praises of Him who called you out of darkness into His marvelous light" (1 Peter 2:9). Paul is equally expressive. "And do not be drunk with wine, in which is dissipation; but be filled with the Spirit, speaking to one another in psalms and hymns and spiritual songs, singing and making melody in your heart to the Lord" (Ephesians 5:18, 19).

It is obvious from these vibrant Christians that the assurance and praise of those filled with the Spirit will be heard in many different ways. As the Spirit bears witness in a life each day and there is a "Abba" relationship with God these feelings will be as impossible to hide as the noonday sun in a cloudless sky. Do you know someone who is having this experience? Do not criticize and condemn if your own heart is unmoved. Rather, remember that "Abba, Father" is constantly drawing His children to Him. I noticed an excellent balance in a pioneer Adventist document. "Now, brethren, be careful and do not go into or try to create human excitement. But while we should be careful not to go into human excitement, we should not be among those who will raise inquiries and cherish doubts in reference to the work of the Spirit of God; for there will be those who will question and criticize when the Spirit of God takes possession of men and women, because their own hearts are not moved, but are cold and unimpressible." [11]

Juanita Kretschmar is a wonderful Christian who directs the prayer-based New York van ministry, helping thousands with practical Christianity on the streets of that huge city. I have heard Juanita a number of times tell the story of her original struggles with God and how God led her again and again to the thought *Ask for the Holy Spirit.* Finally she took her Bible and claimed the promise as given in Luke 11:13. Telling her experience, she says, "I paused. Nothing happened. So I prayed again and again until finally after some 30 minutes I became aware of the Holy Spirit's presence. In my mind's eye I could see the silhouette of three crosses on a distant hill. I saw no person, but I was well aware of that center cross." Juanita went on to describe her experience of deep confession and the wonderful assurance of eternal life. The more she experienced the power of the Spirit, the more she thirsted to know Him. "I got off my knees and walked over to the window of my bedroom. I looked up into the heavens thinking, *I want to see Him. What kind of God is He? He waited so long, so courteously, until I gave Him my attention, until I listened. I want to meet Him, I want to know Him.* . . . I got back on my knees to thank Him and to weep at such love. It was as though for the first time my eyes were opened. I felt free from the need of pretense, the need to put on a facade. I had no idea I had been carrying such a burden all my life. Now I knew I was free. I felt an inner peace." That experience happened more than 20 years ago, but since that day Juanita has continued to share the joy and peace that she found. Her first appointment is with Jesus each morning, asking Him to take possession of her life by the Holy Spirit. As a result of the assurance and joy that grows each day in Juanita's heart, many continue to be led to know Jesus as their Saviour and to give their life to Him. This is not imagination—this is the witness of the Spirit. Abba, Father.

Inner Witness or Imagination?

Cohesive Contrasts

Apart from your own father, who is the most "fatherly" person you have known? What made him special?

When you were small, did you have a special loving name for your father? Would you like to share it with the group?

Consideration of the Word
Study Text: Romans 8:9-16

Many people are uncertain of their earthly father, but what absolute assurance does the Holy Spirit give us of our heavenly Father (Romans 8:14-16)? _____

_____

In the New Testament it was expected that people would know if they were filled with the Holy Spirit (Acts 19:2; 6:3). Why is this certainty so rare among Christians now? *Is certainty of being fill with the Holy Spirit rare? why?*

Modesty _____ Confusion about the topic _____

Lack of Bible study _____ Weak faith _____

Wrong teaching _____ Other _____

Number the following statements from 1 to 7 in the sequence you see these taking place on the basis of our studies in the previous chapters (some may apply more than once—e.g., the step of faith).

Conversion _____ Filled with the Spirit _____ The Holy Spirit with us _____ The step of faith _____ Deep longing for filling _____ Acceptance of Jesus as Saviour _____ The Spirit enters to dwell in us _____

After your thirsting for the Spirit and taking the step of faith, what connection do you see between the witness of the Spirit (Romans 8:16) and the inner witness (1 John 5:6, 10)? _____

_____

_____

As the Spirit convicts you daily that you are a child of God, what is your response? _____

_____

_____

_____

What the _do you see and_ List the qualities of inner strength from the Holy Spirit that you most _from what we read,_ appreciate right now as you read Paul's prayer for the Ephesians (3:14-21). _1st Read_

_____

_____

_____

According to Ephesians 2:7-9 and Titus 3:5, does our salvation in any way depend on feeling? What is your reason? _____

_____

What evidence do you see that our God who saves us by faith has not given His children a feelingless religion? Look at Luke 19:37-40; 24:52, 53; Ephesians 5:18, 19.

_____

_____

In constrast to the true feelings God gives, what are some dangers of "human excitement"? _____

_____

If you have the inner witness of the Spirit and you could put together a public or group event to express how you feel, what sort of things would you include and exclude? Why? _____

_____

_____

I ask some friends if they are children of God and they reply that they don't know. How can I explain to them about the inner witness of the Spirit? _____

_____

_____

Conversation With the Lord

First, in complete surrender and openness to God's will, quietly ask God for the inner witness of His Spirit.

Second, praise God that you are His child. Praise God for what He is doing in your group.

Finally, pray for specific needs that have been expressed—financial, marital, health, work, family, etc.

Close the group meeting with the Lord's Prayer.

Committing the Word to Memory

This week, write out Romans 8:15, 16. Memorize these verses, then share them with someone as soon as possible.

_____

_____

_____

_____

CHAPTER EIGHT

Will Our Neighbors Know?

While some Christians openly proclaim that they are saved and others who are theologically inclined state that they are justified, what do their neighbors, their families, their school and work associates look for? What do you look for in those who emphatically state that they are born again? The answer is simple. Does Christianity really make a difference to a person's life? If my neighbors hear me screaming at my wife, swearing at the cat, or lying to the children collecting money for the Boy Scouts, they are not going to be particularly impressed when I start sharing with them over the back fence about what Jesus has done in my life.

I am interested in forgiveness. My neighbors are interested in seeing in me the evidence of victory. I am interested in justification. They are interested in my sanctification.

This leads to another question. Why *does* God make it possible for Christians to be filled with the Spirit? I have talked to people who felt that the supreme purpose for people being filled with the Spirit is so they can have an exciting time at church, or so they can get on an emotional high, or even for the purpose of working a few miracles. Actually, these are not the real reasons at all.

Notice what Jesus clearly stated to His disciples. "You shall receive power when the Holy Spirit has come upon you; and you shall be witnesses to me in Jerusalem, and in all Judea and Samaria, and to the end of the earth" (Acts 1:8). While there are a number of important reasons that the Holy Spirit was given, witness or service is the primary and paramount reason for the outpouring of the Holy Spirit. All other reasons find their ultimate purpose in this.

Luke in his Gospel has recorded it another way: "Then He said to them, 'Thus it is written, and thus it was necessary for the Christ to suffer and rise from the dead the third day, and that repentance and remission of sins should be preached in His name to all nations, beginning at Jerusalem. And you are witnesses of these things. Behold, I send the Promise of My Father upon you; but tarry in the city of Jerusalem until you are endued with power from on high'" (Luke 24:46-49). Witness without power is futile. Spiritual power without witness is impossible.

We have already noticed Jesus' promise of the Holy Spirit in John 7. "On the last day, that great day of the feast, Jesus stood and cried out, saying, 'If anyone thirsts, let him come to Me and drink. He who believes in Me, as the Scripture has said, out of his heart will flow rivers of living water'" (verses 37, 38). At first we drink of the living water of the Holy Spirit. The result is to be not a human holding tank (to use plumbing terminology), but rather a pipeline through which living water flows to other thirsty people.

On June 20, 1977, the Trans-Alaska $7.7 billion pipeline began carrying oil 789 miles from the Prudhoe Bay oil field to Valdez. When I visited the pipeline recently near Fairbanks, I noticed the careful adjustments that are made so that there can be compensation for the melting of the permafrost foundations. That pipeline does not exist for its own benefit. It is not expensively maintained as a tourist attraction. The oil is not pumped through the pipe just to prove that it can be done as an exciting achievement of modern engineering. The pipeline has a purpose—to deliver oil. The oil has a purpose in transforming the lives of millions by providing power for transportation, heating, and industry.

The pipeline through which the Holy Spirit flows is an open, human life. The pipeline must be clean and functional. This is also the work of the Holy Spirit. Brian was an academy junior whose physical and academic problems brought him into constant conflict. At a special Holy Spirit emphasis weekend on the academy campus Brian was moved by the Holy Spirit to make a commitment for Jesus. Many students who had cared little for religion other than studying it as a course requirement now felt moved by a God that they had not enjoyed since kindergarten Bible class. At summer youth camp Brian was baptized in the cool waters of a beautiful mountain lake. Immediately the camp leaders recognized in Brian abilities that had never before surfaced. He was offered a position as a counselor and began a ministry for fellow youth, which surprised everyone except Brian's God.

According to the New Testament there are two external evidences of the Holy Spirit filling a human life. Look at them in Acts 4. Peter and John were preaching in the Temple when the authorities became upset and

91

threw them into prison (verses 1-3). That is where many Christians are today. They are imprisoned by fears and inhibitions and seem unable to proclaim the love of Jesus effectively or know His victory power. Notice, though, that this chapter includes the infallible key to escape. Peter was filled with the Holy Spirit (verse 8). Now, as always, the two signs become obvious. First, Peter witnessed verbally and audibly about Jesus, concluding that "there is no other name under heaven given among men by which we must be saved" (verses 8-12).

Second, the enemies of Peter and John, the enemies of the gospel, acknowledged that these men had been with Jesus. The reflection of the character of Jesus the enemy saw caused them to marvel. Commenting on this, one writer says, "Christ filled their thoughts; the advancement of His kingdom was their aim. In mind and character they had become like their Master, and men 'took knowledge of them, that they had been with Jesus' (Acts 4:13)." [1]

"Be Like Jesus, This My Song"

You may feel that telling people about Jesus is a difficult task, and you are right, humanly speaking. To reflect the character of Jesus seems worse than difficult—it seems absolutely impossible. When I was a young person, someone told me that to get to heaven I had to reproduce God's character perfectly. I decided I would never make it, and I was right, humanly speaking. Later I discovered to my amazement that the biblical emphasis on obedience, victory, character beauty, and Christlikeness is not the emphasis of threat, but of promise. God is not saying, "You had better obey Me and become like Me or you will not get to heaven." Instead He says, "By My Holy Spirit you will have victory power, and without even realizing what is happening, you will become like Jesus, not to earn salvation but because Jesus has already saved you." Now, that is exciting! It is not my work, but God's. I cooperate with Him and give Him complete permission daily to work in my life and to use me whatever way He chooses.

Look at how the Holy Spirit makes possible the external evidences of His inner presence.

The character of Jesus is summarized in the fruit of the Spirit. "But the fruit of the Spirit is love, joy, peace, longsuffering, kindness, goodness, faithfulness, gentleness, self-control" (Galatians 5:22, 23). Notice in this chapter that Paul compares the fruit of the Spirit to some very diverse works of human nature. "Now the works of the flesh are evident, which are: adultery, fornication, uncleanness, licentiousness, idolatry, sorcery, hatred, contentions, jealousies, outbursts of wrath, selfish ambitions, dissensions, heresies, envy, murders, drunkenness, revelries, and the like; of which I tell you beforehand, just as I also told you in time past, that those who practice such things will not inherit the kingdom of God" (Galatians 5:19-21). James speaks of the fruit of the Spirit as the fruit of righteousness (James 3:18), because it grows out of the right standing born-again Christians have with God through accepting the salvation gift of Jesus. But notice again the comparison of the Spirit-filled life and the selfishness of natural, sinful humanity. "But if you have bitter envy and self-seeking in your hearts, do not boast and lie against the truth. This wisdom does not descend from above, but is earthly, sensual, demonic. For where envy and self-seeking exists, confusion and every evil thing will be there. But the wisdom that is from above is first pure, and peaceable, gentle, willing to yield, full of mercy and good fruits, without partiality and without hypocrisy. Now the fruit of righteousness is sown in peace by those who make peace" (verses 14-18).

Only the miracle-working power of Jesus through the Holy Spirit can make the fruit of the Spirit possible. That is obvious. A young mother who had struggled with bulemia and depression as a college student came close to the breaking point when her severely mentally and physically handicapped child screamed all night for weeks following an operation. In the midst of this the mother played her Bible tape of Acts 4 and, hearing the story of Peter and John, opened her heart finally and fully to Jesus. Daily filling with the Holy Spirit brought victory and joy. The fruit of patience began to flourish in her life. Recently Rita said, "The Spirit has given me a love for God's Word and an eagerness to know Jesus better. I can be sure that God will continue to eradicate sin in my life, because I can see how He has changed me so far. It seems ironic that some people fear emotionalism when we talk about the Holy Spirit, because only since accepting the Spirit's control have I had a consistent walk with God despite the variety of my emotions."

While it is true that the closer we come to Jesus the less likely we are to claim to be like Him, others nevertheless will notice changes that will verify for them our emphasis on the saving grace of Jesus Christ.

Without a doubt the supreme fruitage of the Holy Spirit is unselfish love. Out of love grow joy and peace, along with the other beautiful character qualities listed in Galatians 5. In the midst of his study on the working of the Holy Spirit, Paul included for the Corinthians and for us a major discussion of the preeminence of love. Take time to read 1 Corinthians 13 and notice how love supersedes all gifts or even qualities of character.

How is this fruit of love made possible? Is it manufactured by determined effort, as a mother teaches a child to enjoy vegetables as much as ice cream? No, this love becomes part of our life because, as we open ourselves to the Holy Spirit, God's love is poured into us. "The love of God has been poured out in our hearts by the Holy Spirit who was given to us" (Romans 5:5).

The love of God in us is, in reality, God in us, for "God is love" (1 John 4:16). This fruit of love brings us total stability in Jesus. R. A. Torrey, commenting on Ephesians 3:17, speaks of our being rooted and grounded in love. "Paul therefore was saying that by the strengthening of the Spirit in the inward man we send the roots of our life deep down into the soil of love and also that the foundations of the superstructure of our character are built upon the rock of love. Love is the sign of holiness, the fulfilling of the law (Romans 13:10). Love is what we all need most in our relations to God, to Jesus Christ, and to one another. And it is the work of the Holy Spirit to root and ground our lives in love. There is the most intimate relation between Christ being formed within us, or made to dwell in us, and our being rooted and grounded in love, for Jesus Christ Himself is the absolute perfect embodiment of divine love."[2] Have you ever felt a little unstable in your love relationships in the family, church, or community? The fruit of the Spirit is love, and love is the greatest stabilizing influence of all.

I came from a family situation where love was not expressed in a demonstrative way. No one hugged and said, "I love you." My mother cared for me very well, and her strong faith after becoming a Christian guided me into a close walk with God. But it was not until I experienced the real power of the Holy Spirit that the fruit of expressive love began to be revealed in my life. I had to move from the self-centeredness of an only child to the "love for others" centeredness of a child of God. I have seen this happen in many lives. One mother said to her children after their father had been filled with the Holy Spirit, "Isn't it wonderful to see the change in Daddy?" The children agreed. "Daddy doesn't yell at us like he used to." The children had grown up with a fear of the dark because of a frightening experience the oldest child had experienced years before. "We prayed with our children that they might be filled with the Holy Spirit," the father explained recently. "One evidence of the Spirit's work in their lives was that they lost their fear of the dark." Remember the love of God is poured into hearts by the Holy Spirit and that love casts out fear. What fruit, what joy!

Surprised by a Spiritual Gift

If the fruit of the Spirit is one of the two external signs of the filling of the Holy Spirit, what is the other? The disciples after Pentecost not only revealed the character of Jesus, but spoke and worked for Him in many practical ways. When people are filled with the Spirit, they will not only strongly desire to reflect Jesus' character, but also be on fire for the enlargement of His kingdom. They will want to work for Jesus so that His love and truth can be spread to as many as possible.

Steve was a young Christian who loved the Lord but felt a void in his experience. As he began to read an old book on the Holy Spirit, he realized that the Holy Spirit was the answer that filled the void in ways he had never expected. At a camp meeting Steve attended a class on the Holy Spirit led by Spirit-filled pastor Kevin Wilfley. There Steve noticed how people at the end of each class began to praise God as they told of changes in their lives. Small groups prayed. Problems dissolved, and love, joy, and peace became a reality in people's lives. "We began to live," Steve exclaimed, "under the power of God's Spirit dwelling within us." Not only did Steve see changes within his life, such as not holding grudges toward those who hurt him, but he discovered that his desire to share his faith gradually helped overcome his natural shyness. "There are exciting changes in my life," Steve said recently as he talked of the influence of the Spirit within him. "Boredom is totally foreign to me now. My greatest desire is to serve my Creator and my fellow men and to share eternal life with them all."

I spoke recently to two Spirit-filled attorneys in different parts of the country who had turned from law practice into full-time gospel ministry. A trucking manufacturer has been convicted to give millions to gospel work in Third World and Eastern European countries. A young mother began Neighborhood Home Bible Studies with five or six people on her block. A physician opened his office as a center for small group studies in practical Christianity. A college student organized 24 fellowship groups on his campus. Two academy juniors led Scripture studies in the suburb where the academy is located. An elderly lady found she could give encouragement and spiritual strength to the residents of a nursing home. A single parent held a weekly Bible class for primaries that none of those children would think of missing. A recovering alcoholic ministered in a weekly support group that brought new victories and hope to a half dozen families.

It appears from Scripture that each born-again Christian receives one or more special ministry gifts from God. These ministry gifts are in addition to the natural talent that every Christian can use in God's service. Peter said, "As each one has received a gift, minister it to one another, as good stewards of the manifold grace of God" (1 Peter 4:10). While this may refer to natural and supernatural gifts, Paul is more specific regarding the supernatural endowment of the spiritual gifts when he admonishes Timothy not to neglect but rather to stir up the gift that was given to him when Paul and the elders laid hands on him (1 Timothy 4:14; 2 Timothy 1:6). In Romans 12, 1 Corinthians 12, and Ephesians 4 the emphasis is specifically on spiritual gifts. Apparently, just as from earthly parents natural talents originate, so from the Holy Spirit spiritual gifts originate. Just as after birth natural talents gradually become obvious, so after the new birth spiritual gifts become increasingly plain.

It is clear that no one gift is in itself the sign of the Holy Spirit. "Now there are diversities of gifts, but the same Spirit. There are differences of ministries, but the same Lord. And there are diversities of activities, but it is the same God who works all in all" (1 Corinthians 12:4-6). A Spirit-filled Christian is open to the leading of the Holy Spirit because "one and the same Spirit works all these things, distributing to each one individually as He wills" (verse 11).

The Holy Spirit gives as He wills, not as we want. In Romans 12 Paul emphasizes that the gifts differ according to the grace given us. Various instruments have been developed to enable Christians to find these spiritual gifts. Some of these instruments have resulted in people misusing the biblical teaching of spiritual gifts. One church member who refused to support the church financially said that giving was not his spiritual gift. He did, however, claim the gift of administration and wanted to run the church. Another who gave a scathing rebuke to a brother said he had the gift of prophecy but at the same time did not claim to have the gift of mercy. Some refused to share in the outreach of the church, stating that they had the gift of prayer.

While distortions may seem disturbing, we should not find them discouraging. Nothing is more exciting and rewarding than discovering and using your spiritual gifts. Paul says to desire spiritual gifts. Prayerfully consider the three lists of spiritual gifts (Romans 12; 1 Corinthians 12;

Ephesians 4), asking God to help you understand which gifts He has miraculously given you. Ask counsel from spiritual friends and church leaders. Try a number of different types of ministries until your gift becomes apparent. While you will major in ministry within the area of your spiritual gifts, do not in any way use this as an excuse not to use your other talents and abilities to fulfill the broad scope of Christian responsibility.

One of the best helps in discovering your spiritual gifts has been developed by Dr. Roy Naden, professor of religious education at Andrews University. Naden sees six gift clusters: the support cluster, counselor cluster, teacher cluster, shepherd evangelist cluster, leader cluster, and sign cluster. No doubt you will discover your spiritual gift or gifts within one or more of these clusters. [3]

William McRae in his *Dynamics of Spiritual Gifts* is helpful when he outlines the four features embodied in every spiritual gift. [4] First, he says, there will be ability. A successful pastor recently stated that he does not have the gift of pastoring, but rather leadership and preaching. How then does he pastor his rapidly growing church? Many of his members have the gift of pastoring, so he equips them and organizes them as small group leaders. They flourish, the church flourishes, and so does the pastor.

The second feature involved in spiritual gifts, according to McRae, is qualification. One is qualified to lead the choir as a spiritual ministry not just by the talent of music, but rather by a spiritual gift of service. A Vacation Bible School teacher is qualified not by having the time, but rather by having a desire to see the salvation of the children and being able to communicate this effectively in love.

The third feature that McRae lists is strength. It seems that the individual with a spiritual gift will display a strength in the area of that gift that will amaze all onlookers. As an 18-year-old carpentry apprentice I had no idea what my spiritual gift could be. I was extremely nervous as a public speaker and was more inclined to reading and literature. When our pastor asked me to preach, I was shocked, but with much prayer I accepted his invitation. As soon as I began to speak, the gift was revealed, resulting in a ministry that has enabled me to preach to large and small audiences in many countries. Sometimes I have preached a dozen times or more each week for many months, giving evidence of the strength that even to me is unexplainable apart from the power of God.

The final point McRae makes is responsibility. We are responsible for not only our spiritual gifts but all the natural endowments we can use to further God's kingdom and serve humanity. Our oldest daughter, Carolyn, has always given evidence of a natural teaching ability. Even before she attended school she would line up cats, dogs, and dolls and expound to them on topics she knew little more about than her class. Soon she had neighborhood children gathered to instruct them carefully in matters she had begun to learn in school herself. Today she is a successful college teacher. But is this natural endowment also utilized by God as a spiritual gift? Apparently so, as each week Carolyn and her husband, Struan, lead a youth Sabbath school class that has changed the lives of numerous young people. Here is an illustration of a secular talent that God has utilized as a spiritual gift. On the other hand, Struan has a spiritual gift for musical composition and performance that has reached a fairly secularized segment of young society, leading many unchurched youth to take a deeply interested look at the claims of Christianity and the love of Jesus. Sometimes his group practices late into the night, showing that extra strength that enables him to fulfill the responsibility of these gifts.

Will our neighbors know whether or not our claim to Christianity and Holy Spirit power is really valid? The fruit and gifts of the Spirit will provide an answer. These two external evidences will bear witness, as will the inner witness of our hearts.

One final point concerning ministry. Not only does the Holy Spirit give the sense of mission I need for my life, along with the graces and gifts to meet that mission, but the reverse is also true. When I face what I consider a missionless day (for instance, a day off my usual routine of work, when I am just going to read the newspaper and do a few jobs around the house and garden), that is the day I seem to be the least motivated to pray for the Spirit. I just get out of bed a little later than usual and quite unintentionally roll on into the day. I always feel a sense of loss when this happens, but for many people, every day is like that. There is no sense of mission, no sense of spiritual ministry, so there is little motivation to pray.

It is for this reason that churches that are most on fire with the Holy Spirit usually have multiplied ministries for their members and especially small group ministries where as many as possible can be involved. Take time today to evaluate your spiritual ministry. Ask God, if it is not already obvious, to lead you into a ministry that will give you a daily purpose for prayer beyond your own personal necessities. Within that ministry the fruit of the Holy Spirit and the gifts of the Spirit will flourish and ripen into a daily harvest of joy.

Will Our Neighbors Know?

Cohesive Contrasts

Group members minister to each other in many special ways. This leads us into an "affirmation" sharing time, which is always very positive.

Tell of one positive way each group member has encouraged and blessed your life.

Consideration of the Word
Study Text: Acts 4:1-13

Previous to this study, what did you feel was the main reason for God giving the filling of the Holy Spirit (A)? What reason do you now see as most important (B)? Mark (A) and (B) on the list below and tell the group what this change of understanding (if any) means to you.

Good feelings _____ Excitement in church _____

Witness and outreach _____ Emotional high _____

Miracles _____ Bring tears _____ Other _____

What could be some reasons for the close connection between the power of the Holy Spirit and our witness for Jesus (Acts 1:8; John 7:37, 38)? _____

_____

_____

_____

Read again the story of Peter and John in Acts 4:1-13. How did the enemies of the gospel see in the words and lives of these men the evidence of Peter and John being filled with the Holy Spirit (verses 8-13)? _____

_____

_____

Even the enemies of Peter and John recognized in them clear indications that they had become like Jesus. Do you feel excited, dumbfounded, or doubtful about your possibility of reflecting the character of Jesus? Why? _____

_____

_____

To witness for Jesus while revealing to others the ugliness of our sinful nature can be very negative. How does the fruit of the Spirit enable Christians to be like Jesus (Galatians 5:22, 23; James 3:15-18)? _____

_____

_____

The fruit of true Christian love is a miracle of the Holy Spirit. List some ways you see God's love stabilizing your Christian experience (Ephesians 3:17).

_____

_____

_____

What external special spiritual talents or gifts enabled Peter and John to witness and how effective were they (Acts 4:2, 4)? _____

_____

_____

Apparently, as well as natural talents received at birth, each born-again Christian receives a spiritual gift (1 Peter 4:2). Have you recognized your spiritual gift yet? If so, share with the group how this recognition came. _____

_____

_____

If you have not yet recognized your gift, begin by praying through 1 Corinthians 12; Romans 12; Ephesians 4. Ask others what gifts they see in you. What indications do you find in 1 Corinthians 12:4-11 that not all Spirit-filled Christians are given the same gifts? _____

_____

_____

If you discovered right now a gift that you did not previously see in yourself, what steps would you take to begin to use the gift? For example, the gift of pastoring, prayer, healing, evangelism, administration, giving. _____

_____

_____

Conversation With the Lord

Continue to affirm each other in prayer, but first, affirm God—praise and bless God.

Second, thank God for special gifts you see in group members, and pray for opportunities to use gifts in outreach and nurture ministry.

Third, pray for felt needs inside and outside the group.

Remember to conclude by praying the Lord's Prayer together.

Committing the Word to Memory

This week, write out Acts 4:13. Memorize this verse, then share it with someone as soon as possible.

_____

_____

_____

Greater Works Than Jesus'

"Expect a miracle," the song said, and the group that vigorously sang these words sounded so vibrant and enthusiastic that I looked around expecting the unexpected to happen at any moment. Modern education in the Western scientific method has led the world into a skepticism of miracles that has caused many to doubt God and reject the supernatural. Nevertheless, have you noticed the pendulum swinging the other way recently? Not only are miracles believable, but many people are convinced that they can be expected today on a regular basis. Why is this? Perhaps it is because we have become accustomed to electronic phenomena, which are almost miraculous (except to a few technicians who have combined scientific principles with natural laws).

At a beautiful retreat center up in California's San Bernardino Mountains I was speaking to an Asian group about the omnipresence of the Holy Spirit. At the start of the meeting I noticed a young man with a Walkman radio and earphones, and called him forward and explained that the air around us was full of sounds and pictures. It seemed unbelievable as we looked up from the outdoor amphitheater into the clear night sky. But as we noticed with that Walkman, with the right receiver a whole radio or television broadcast could be received. To someone living 150 years ago it would have seemed impossible or miraculous, but to the 200 people in the group that night it was completely believable. "We don't each receive a 200th part of the picture of events in the Middle East," I explained, "but with the correct receiver we can all get the whole picture right out of the clear sky."

Perhaps some miracles can be explained by laws known to God, or maybe He occasionally supersedes natural laws. However impossible real miracles are to explain, there is no doubt that they happen. I like Peter Wagner's definition: "The gift of miracles is the special ability that God gives to certain members of the body of Christ to serve as human intermediaries through whom it pleases God to perform powerful acts that are perceived by observers to have altered the ordinary course of nature." [1] Wagner goes on to say that this definition does not close the door to later scientific explanations, but it recognizes the fact that God can and does choose to work by the Holy Spirit in many ways that to human minds today, and possibly always, will be totally unexplainable.

Miracle Ministry

Although miracles are recorded a number of times in the Old Testament, only three main clusters appear. The times of the Exodus, Elijah and Elisha, and Daniel were marked by significant supernatural activity. But even these great events pale into insignificance compared with the miracle-working ministry of Jesus. Some of the 35 specifically mentioned miracles of Jesus are summarized when John the Baptist's disciples came to inquire about the authenticity of Jesus as the Messiah. "And that very hour He cured many people of their infirmities, afflictions, and evil spirits; and to many who were blind He gave sight. Then Jesus answered and said to them, 'Go and tell John the things you have seen and heard: that the blind see, the lame walk, the lepers are cleansed, the deaf hear, the dead are raised, the poor have the gospel preached to them' " (Luke 7:21, 22).

About 100 times the New Testament tells of signs, wonders, and amazing events that surrounded Jesus. Hebrews clearly attributes these supernatural occurrences to the working of the Holy Spirit. "God also bearing witness both with signs and wonders, with various miracles, and gifts of the Holy Spirit, according to His own will" (Hebrews 2:4).

Now for the stunning news. As Jesus prepared His disciples for His departure, He made an incredible promise. "Most assuredly, I say to you, he who believes in Me, the works that I do he will do also; and greater works than these will he do, because I go to My Father" (John 14:12). How were the disciples to do the works of Jesus and even greater? Among the 30 promises Jesus made in John 14-16, He emphasized at least four times that the Holy Spirit would be the source and center of all the disciples' ministry (John 14:16, 17, 26; 15:24; 16:7-15). Mark records Jesus' promise to His disciples of miracle-working power (Mark 16:17, 18).

Look at some of the dramatic miracles that the disciples witnessed. The lame man was healed in Jerusalem (Acts 3); all sick and devil possessed people brought into the presence of the disciples were healed

(Acts 5); there were signs and wonders in Iconium (Acts 14); handkerchiefs and aprons from Paul brought healing from disease and evil spirits (Acts 19).

Even in the time of the disciples people wanted the miracle-working power of God to use for their own purposes. There always seems to be someone ready to exploit the supernatural. Simon, the baptized Samaritan, was amazed when he saw the miracles and signs that Philip did under the power of God (Acts 8:13). Later he tried to purchase the power of the Holy Spirit with money because he no doubt saw the Holy Spirit as the giver of supernatural power (verses 18, 19).

Although Simon was wrong in his motives he was right about the source of power. To the Romans Paul says, "In mighty signs and wonders, by the power of the Spirit of God, so that from Jerusalem and round about Illyricum I have fully preached the gospel of Christ" (Romans 15:19). In his letter to the Galatians Paul linked the Holy Spirit and miracles to faith. "Therefore He who supplies the Spirit to you and works miracles among you, does He do it by the works of the law, or by the hearing of faith?" (Galatians 3:5). Paul's ministry was a demonstration of the Holy Spirit and power (1 Corinthians 2:4). This enabled him to work "signs and wonders and mighty deeds" (2 Corinthians 12:12).

The evidence of the miracle-working power of the Holy Spirit is overwhelming. But perhaps you may wonder if it was only for the 11 disciples plus Paul. No, remember that Philip worked miracles at Samaria (Acts 8:13) and was a Spirit-filled deacon (Acts 6:5). Barnabas had the gift of encouragement (Acts 11:22-24), but he also shared in miracle-working ministry (Acts 14:3).

Are Miracles Obsolete?

Now the question naturally arises: Were such gifts as miracles and healing given only to get the early Christian church started? I do not believe so, and I have some good reasons for that. But first let us look at the biblical evidence. In Paul's listing of spiritual gifts in 1 Corinthians 12 he mentions healing and miracles among such others as preaching and administration. Earlier in this same letter he said, "So that you come short in no gift, eagerly waiting for the revelation of our Lord Jesus Christ, who will also confirm you to the end, that you may be blameless in the day of our Lord Jesus Christ" (1 Corinthians 1:7, 8). Apparently no gift was to be absent from those who wait for the return of Jesus.

James encourages those who are waiting for the coming of the Lord, and clearly directs them to anoint the sick with oil while praying for their healing. "Therefore be patient, brethren, until the coming of the Lord. See how the farmer waits for the precious fruit of the earth, waiting patiently for it until it receives the early and latter rain. . . . Is any among you suffering? Let him pray. Is anyone cheerful? Let him sing psalms. Is anyone among you sick? Let him call for the elders of the church, and let them pray over him, anointing him with oil in the name of the Lord. And the prayer of faith will save the sick, and the Lord will raise him up. And if he has committed sins, he will be forgiven. Confess your trespasses to one another, and pray for one another, that you may be healed. The effective, fervent prayer of a righteous man avails much" (James 5:7-16). If miracles were beneficial in the establishment of Christianity, how much more important will they be as the church is involved in the intense struggle preceding the return of Jesus.

Two events absolutely convinced me of the certainty of miracles in the twentieth century. As a teenager I became acquainted with W. E. Minns, a sincere lay leader in his local church congregation. I did not belong to any church, and was very impressed with Mr. Minns' knowledge of the Bible as he studied the teachings of Scripture with my mother and me in our home. I soon learned an amazing experience that had taken place in this man's life about two years earlier. W. E. Minns had been diagnosed as having cancer of the liver, and when the surgeons operated they found the cancer was terminal and in the final stages. Mr. Minns returned home and was able some weeks later to attend a Christian camp meeting, where a day of special fasting and prayer brought many people together to intercede for this man of God. After the anointing with oil according to instructions in James 5, Mr. Minns was convinced that the Lord had healed him. Was it true? Had it really happened? Subsequent medical tests showed, to the amazement of the physicians and surgeons, that he now had the completely healthy liver of a young man. No scientific theory could explain this remarkable change. W. E. Minns lived another 35 active years as a remarkable testimony of the miracle-working power of God.

Mr. Minns' life and experience affected me in a number of ways I did not expect. Not only did I decide to accept the Lord into my life and be baptized into Mr. Minns' congregation, but by the time I was 21 years old I was very sick myself. Increasingly severe internal pain over a number of months led me to seek medical help. Tests revealed that I had a large duodenal ulcer that refused to heal even when treated with various medications and diet. This condition eventually worsened through scar tissue blocking the pylorus. Surgery could possibly have alleviated this condition through the removal of part of the stomach and duodenum, but I did not feel at all positive about such action at only 21 years of age. Gradually I became weaker, until I did not even have the strength to dry myself after a bath or shower. It was in this condition that I recalled the experience of W. E. Minns, and there was for the first time in months a ray of hope that beamed into my heart and mind.

I still remember vividly the day of prayer and anointing. My church pastor, Eric Robinson; W. E. Minns; and a number of other church elders participated. As I was anointed, I felt as if an electric current had passed through me, and I knew instantly that I was healed. The next day after the anointing some members of that church congregation were helping a family who had lost their home in a fire build a new house. While visiting the construction site, I found, to my amazement and the astonishment of all present, that I was able to lift and carry two very heavy bags of cement. This was only one day after being so weak that I had to be helped into the church. A few days later I visited my physician, who ordered several X-rays and tests. "I am an atheist," he said in his strong Scottish accent. "But what I see here I must admit is a miracle. There is not even any evidence of scar tissue." Yes, I do believe in miracles, and I am sure now you can see why.

There was another wonderful outcome of all of this in my life. A few months after my healing one of Mr. Minns' daughters, Barbara, became my wife, and together through the years we have seen God work miracles in our lives and in the lives of others. As a pastor I have prayed for many who have been healed. On the other hand, I have prayed for many more who have not been healed, which has, I have discovered, been harder for some to accept than miracles.

When Miracles Don't Happen

This brings us to the question of praying according to God's will. "Now this is the confidence that we have in Him, that if we ask anything according to His will, He hears us" (1 John 5:14). Some people feel that to ask according to God's will is a sign of weakness and lack of faith. To others it seems a human attempt to force God into action if we do not ask according to His will. I take the latter position, but remember well one occasion when I met a man who took the first position very seriously. I was selling Christian books and was asked to visit the home of a very wealthy businessman. He was not interested in buying books, but was anxious that I pray for him. We knelt on the plush carpet in the luxurious living room as I prayed concerning his Parkinson's disease. "Lord, I ask that Your will will be done," I said earnestly in the middle of my prayer. Instantly Mr. Farrah jumped to his feet and asked me to leave his house. "I don't want such lack of faith here," he shouted. "Of course it is God's will to heal me."

Although healing is always God's will, it does not necessarily come in this life. Sometimes it will come on the day of resurrection, when there will be no more sickness, pain, or death. When we do witness healing now we taste a little of the power of the age to come (Hebrews 6:5). Even Paul, with his marvelous gift of healing, did not receive healing himself. "Concerning this thing I pleaded with the Lord three times that it might depart from me. And He said to me, 'My grace is sufficient for you, for My strength is made perfect in weakness.' Therefore most gladly I will rather boast in my infirmities, that the power of Christ may rest upon me" (2 Corinthians 12:8, 9). To Timothy Paul wrote that "Trophimus I have left in Miletus sick" (2 Timothy 4:20). And yet Trophimus came from Ephesus, where "God worked unusual miracles by the hand of Paul, so that even handkerchiefs or aprons were brought from his body to the sick, and the diseases left them and the evil spirits went out of them" (Acts 19:11, 12). So not even Paul could heal himself or others according to his own will.

Sometimes people who are not healed after special prayer become depressed because they are made to feel lacking in faith. This is not true. Paul had tremendous faith and yet was not healed. On the other hand, Jesus healed some seemingly rather faithless people. The fact also remains true that even those with the strongest faith have all eventually died and await the wonderful day when this "corruptible has put on incorruption, and this mortal must put on immortality" (1 Corinthians 15:53).

What place do miracles have in the experience of Christians today? Would you like a miracle right now? A man who emphatically stated that he did not believe in miracles as God's present method of working rushed into my office one day and asked me to pray for his wife, who had been admitted into intensive care at the local hospital. I felt inclined to ask him if he now believed in miracles, but instead I prayed earnestly for his wife's recovery. Jesus indicated that signs and miracles would follow those who believed (Mark 16:17). Even with the disciples miracles were not pushed into the forefront. In fact, Jesus said that an evil and adulterous generation asks for a sign (Matthew 12:39).

Signs and miracle seekers are plentiful today looking for a quick religious thrill and Christian showmanship. Whenever miracles are discussed, someone will always say, "Don't you know, Satan exploits and counterfeits miracles, so we have to be very careful." Someone else says, "It is dangerous to pray for miracles or healing. This is what Jim Jones did, and look where it led the people who followed him. Jim Bakker prayed for signs and wonders, and he ended up in prison." I am well aware of the dangers and will talk about spiritual warfare in the next chapter, but counterfeits are always an indication that the true is present and possible. If we become intimidated by false religion, we will be forced to reject nearly all parts of Christianity, because most good is somewhere exploited for evil. It is certainly true of prayer, preaching, and pastoral ministry. Church offerings and counseling have been misused. No Spirit-filled Christian would suggest, however, that these vital parts of Christianity be rejected or eliminated. I have come to the same conclusion about miracles. I believe the true can happen and is happening with increasing rapidity.

It is thrilling to hear what God is doing in China, for instance. In Hong Kong I spoke to some young men from Shanghai who were attending my seminar. Their Spirit-filled ministry is incredible. Samuel Young has reported that Christians in China are opening their homes to their neighbors for Bible study and prayer, that miracles are taking place, that the sick are being healed and devils cast out. [2]

This will happen with increasing frequency in the future. A writer with a vision of final events before the return of Jesus has this to say: "Servants of God, with their faces lighted up and shining with holy consecration, will hasten from place to place to proclaim the message from heaven. By thousands of voices, all over the earth, the warning will be given. Miracles will be wrought, the sick will be healed, and signs and wonders will follow the believers." [3] "In the visions of the night, representation passed before me of a great reformatory movement among God's people. Many were praising God. The sick were healed, and other miracles were wrought. A spirit of intercession was seen, even as was manifest before the great Day of Pentecost. Hundreds and thousands were seen visiting families and opening before them the Word of God. Hearts were converted by the power of the Holy Spirit, and a spirit of genuine conversion was manifest. [4]

The greatest miracle of all takes place when a person is converted and a life radically changed by the power of the Holy Spirit. As the song says: "I believe in miracles, I've seen a soul set free." I am praying that you have known this miracle in your own life. You may have not experienced a healing miracle, but if you have been born again, you will have a faith in true miracles that is unshakable because you have experienced at least one in your own life. A young man told me of his journey into alcoholism and drug abuse. In the midst of this a friend introduced him to Jesus. Today José's life is so radically changed that he leads a small group Bible study and is preparing for full-time gospel ministry. Ben was a boxer who often practiced on his wife. Naomi was beaten by this man who would come home and jeer at the Christian lady who cared for him so well. All her prayers and Bible studies bore fruit, however, when her husband, Ben Green, was miraculously converted and became a successful gospel evangelist leading many to Jesus through the power of the Holy Spirit. "Therefore, if anyone is in Christ, he is a new creation; old things have passed away; behold, all things have become new" (2 Corinthians 5:17).

When William was director of the mission aviation school at Andrews University, he received a call to New Guinea to train and certify pilots in a part of the world where in some areas the beauty of nature is host to many tropical diseases. William's wife, Sue, became desperately ill with dengue fever, which led to bouts of encephalitis, or inflamation of the brain lining, and chronic Epstein-Barr virus. These diseases left Sue in constant pain, barely able to move her head and unable even to hold a pen in her fingers. Returning to the States and settling in Oregon, Sue and William experienced three years of suffering that left them exhausted and discouraged. At a pastors' Holy Spirit Fellowship Sue requested prayer and anointing, and after a day of fasting and prayer we gathered in the evening to participate in this special service. We sang and prayed and quietly claimed many Bible promises. After I had anointed Sue and many pastors and their spouses had laid their hands upon her, we felt at peace, and soon our meeting concluded. Many had returned to their rooms for the night when Ruthie Jacobsen came into the meeting room where a few of us remained. "Sue has been healed," she informed us in a voice that expressed the amazement and praise that we all felt.

The next day Sue told her story. "When the oil was placed on my head during the anointing service, I knew something was happening," she said as we all listened with the reverent wonder of people who had witnessed a miracle. "I could lift my head backwards more than a couple inches—no pain." To demonstrate, she shook her head in a way that would have almost killed her the day before. "The next morning at 5:00 a.m. I was wide awake feeling alive. I was full of praise to God. Now I discovered new things I can do again."

"This morning we went out for a five-mile walk," William said as he praised God. "I could hardly keep up with her." Later tests confirmed Sue's healing, and many have been led to a deeper faith in God from her positive testimony. We are not sure who it was in that gathering that had the special gift of healing by the Holy Spirit; all we know is that once again God chose to work in a miraculous way.

Yes, you can believe in miracles, because you have a miracle-working God. As Jesus promised, by the presence and power of the Holy Spirit His followers will be able to do the works that Jesus did, and even greater because He will enable them to share in His miracle-working power everywhere in the world. Do not underestimate what your potential may be when you and God team up today for service.

Greater Works Than Jesus'

Cohesive Contrasts

There are five levels of communication in a small group: (1) cliché conversation, (2) reporting facts, (3) ideas and judgments, (4) feelings and emotions, (5) openness and personal commitment.

According to the level at which you feel most comfortable, briefly share with the group the greatest miracle you have experienced.

Consideration of the Word
Study Text: Luke 4:16-30

Do you consider miracles harder or easier to believe now than in Bible times? Why? _____

_____

_____

Of the different types of spiritual and physical miracles Jesus was able to perform through the Holy Spirit (Luke 4:18, 19), which is most important to humanity now? Why is this? _____

_____

_____

In the light of Jesus' tremendous miracle-working ability (Luke 7:21, 22), what is your reaction to His promise that His followers will do the same works and even greater (John 14:12)?

Doubt _____ Unbelief _____ Surprise _____

_____

Excitement _____ Caution _____ Faith _____

Other _____

Jesus' claim to fulfill the prophecy of miracle-working ministry led the people of His town to want to kill Him. If you offered to pray for a miracle in your own community, school, or workplace, what do you think the reaction would be? .

_____

_____

Paul mentions miracles and healing among the gifts in 1 Corinthians 12. Do you see significance in His claim that those who wait for the return of Jesus will come short on no gift (1 Corinthians 1:7, 8)? _____

_____

_____

What lessons can we learn from the fact that Paul, who worked many healing miracles, was not healed himself, neither did he heal Trophimus (2 Timothy 4:20)? _____

_____

_____

Praying that God's will be done (1 John 5:14) as we ask for healing could be

Lack of faith _____ A face-saving device _____ An indication of trust _____ Acknowledgment that God knows best _____ A sign of weakness _____ Other _____

If you and a friend pray for a miracle and your friend's prayer receives a positive answer and yours does not, how do you feel?

Unhappy _____ Full of praise _____ Jealous _____

Grateful _____ Hurt _____ Puzzled _____

Patient _____ Trusting _____ Other _____

Christianity began with power and miracles (e.g., Romans 15:19; Galatians 3:5). Why should Christians not allow counterfeits or modern spiritual deceptions to stop them from praying for and experiencing Holy Spirit power and miracles today?

_____

_____

_____

Rewrite in your own words Jesus' promise in Luke 4:18, applying each part of the promise specifically to the miracle of conversion and victory power of the Holy Spirit. (You may need to use another piece of paper.)

_____

_____

_____

_____

Conversation With the Lord

Is there a miracle you would like your group to pray for right now? Ask in faith according to God's will.

For the sick you can follow the advice given in James 5.

Expect a miracle. If God sees that it is best, it will happen. Let each group member have a spirit of deep repentance and surrender to God. Praise Him in faith.

Close as usual with the Lord's Prayer.

Committing the Word to Memory

This week, write out Luke 4:18. Memorize this verse, then share it with someone as soon as possible.

_____

_____

_____

_____

_____

Discerning and Defeating the Enemy

It is paradoxical that while Spirit-filled Christians have been promised peace they are often in the midst of conflict. Equally unexplainable is the fact that these same Christians surrounded by conflict have a peace, humanly speaking, that passes all understanding. Peace for those who are full of the Holy Spirit is not primarily a feeling or a condition, but a person. Jesus is the Prince of Peace—Yahweh-shalom. Jesus summarized this strange coexistence of peace and conflict in the lives of His followers when He said, "These things I have spoken to you that in Me you may have peace. In the world you will have tribulation; but be of good cheer, I have overcome the world" (John 16:33).

Sources of Conflict

No dimension of life matures long without the realization of conflict becoming painfully clear. This world obviously is a war zone, a combat zone. The outward expressions of warfare are only external evidences of the intense spiritual battle that has encompassed the world since evil shattered the tranquillity of Eden. "For we do not wrestle against flesh and blood, but against principalities, against powers, against the rulers of the darkness of this age, against spiritual hosts of wickedness in the heavenly places" (Ephesians 6:12).

Julie sobbed as she talked to me on the phone. "Mike and I have been married only six months and we've had a terrible argument. He is so selfish. I can't bring myself even to speak to him." Julie and Mike so much wanted to serve the Lord. What would happen now? Arthur had pledged a large sum of money to the church building fund. When the news broke that he was declared bankrupt Arthur was rather bitter. "Unfair and dishonest trade practices by my competitors did this to me," he said angrily. "The devil has done all he can to ruin me, and now it looks as if he will be successful."

Was Julie right in saying that trouble was the result of inner evil, or does it come as Arthur suggests—from the work of the devil? Actually, according to the Bible, spiritual warfare must be fought on at least two fronts. I know that is not very comforting, but it is a reality. Here is Paul facing the inner battle. "But I see another law in my members, warring against the law of my mind, and bringing me into captivity to the law of sin which is in my members. O wretched man that I am! Who will deliver me from this body of death?" (Romans 7:23, 24). James also speaks of the war within. "Where do wars and fights come from among you? Do they not come from your desires for pleasure that war in your members?" (James 4:1). Peter admits that there are "fleshly lusts which war against the soul" (1 Peter 2:11). You know of this battle as well as I do. The war is real. We fight every day. Even the most devoted Christians lose a battle occasionally, but in the overall conflict we can say, "But thanks be to God who gives us the victory through our Lord Jesus Christ" (1 Corinthians 15:57).

The other area of warfare we face is external. "Be sober, be vigilant; because your adversary the devil walks about like a roaring lion, seeking whom he may devour" (1 Peter 5:8). Notice the reason for this present intensity. "Therefore rejoice, O heavens, and you who dwell in them! Woe to the inhabitants of the earth and the sea! For the devil has come down to you, having great wrath, because he knows that he has a short time" (Revelation 12:12). I found it helpful when I discovered that "short time" can be translated "limited time." When Satan and his angels were cast out of heaven (verse 9), he still believed that he as a superior angel would be forever triumphant on earth. But he was defeated by the blood of Jesus. "Inasmuch then as the children have partaken of flesh and blood, He Himself likewise shared in the same, that through death He might destroy him who had the power of death, that is, the devil" (Hebrews 2:14). The devil knows now he has only a limited time left to tear apart human lives so he works with vicious intensity. His subtlety is such that he can lead people to think they are serving God when they are under his control.

Discerning the Deceptions

Before we discuss the weapons we can use for constant victory in this internal and external warfare, let us unmask some of the deceptions of satanic forces. We notice that there is a concentrated endeavor to counterfeit the work of the Holy Spirit when at the same time the forces of evil go contrary to the Holy Spirit's ministry. In fact, the devil and his angels work as unholy spirits, disrupting individual lives and whole nations with constant conflict. This is exactly the opposite of the Holy Spirit's ministry of peace, hope, and comfort. Unholy spirits lull unconverted and cultural Christians into a blissful sleepiness and self-satisfaction, which is also the opposite of the Holy Spirit's work of convicting of sin, leading into all truth and glorifying Jesus.

On top of all of this, the enemy loves to practice apparently supernatural trickery. Jesus warned, "For false christs and false prophets will rise and show signs and wonders to deceive, if possible, even the elect" (Mark 13:22). "He performs great signs, so that he even makes fire come down from heaven on the earth in the sight of man. And he deceives those who dwell on the earth by those signs which he was granted to do in the sight of the beast, telling those who dwell on the earth to make an image to the beast who was wounded by the sword and lived" (Revelation 13:13, 14). The majority of the world is so deceived by these deceptions that they are apparently led into the great battle of Armageddon. "For they are spirits of demons, performing signs, which go out to the kings of the earth and of the whole world, to gather them to the battle of that great day of God Almighty" (Revelation 16:14).

In the New Testament "signs" is the same word as "miracles." The result of false signs or miracles is absolutely tragic. Notice how Paul explained this. "The coming of the lawless one is according to the working of Satan, with all power, signs, and lying wonders, and with all unrighteous deception among those who perish, because they did not receive the love of the truth, that they might be saved" (2 Thessalonians 2:9, 10).

I can remember when I first read all these fearful statements and wondered how in the world I could be safe and not be deceived. Listen. God is almighty—He is El-Shaddai. Even while He is allowing the devil to work out his own destruction and demonstrate his irreversibly evil nature, God gives His people all that they need to be completely safe. Did you notice that Paul emphasized in 2 Thessalonians that those who are deceived by Satan's false signs and wonders are those who "did not receive the love of the truth"? That is why it is so important to let the Holy Spirit lead you into all truth (John 16:13). The Holy Spirit is the Spirit of truth. Daily we open our Bibles, study, and pray for the Spirit's leading so we will be led into not only understanding but loving the true teachings of God's Word. This is not a burden; it is a safety. The captors of a hostage in the Middle East gave him food containing arsenic. To have been able to read a label listing ingredients would have been a safeguard, not a burden, for the unsuspecting hostage.

Satan tries to keep us from truth so we can be poisoned by deception. Sometimes people tell us that they have the movings of the Holy Spirit in their meetings, but John indicates the necessity for caution before accepting with open arms all that professes to be from God. "Beloved, do not believe every spirit, but test the spirits, whether they are of God; because many false prophets have gone out into the world" (1 John 4:1). Apparently great numbers will be deceived by false manifestations of spirits, according to Paul's warning regarding events near the end of the world. "Now the spirit expressly says that in the latter time some will depart from the faith, giving heed to deceiving spirits and doctrines of demons" (1 Timothy 4:1).

No wonder the Bible stresses our need to test all spiritual phenomena by truth. The ancient prophet Isaiah gave an enduring test for safety against evil spirits: "And when they say to you, 'Seek those who are mediums and wizards, who whisper and mutter,' should not a people seek their God? Should they seek the dead on behalf of the living? To the law and to the testimony! If they do not speak according to this word, it is because there is no light in them" (Isaiah 8:19, 20). There is no light in anything that is contrary to the witness of God's Word of truth or commandments of Scripture. Even if an apparent miracle or prophecy is accurate and unexplainable, it is no indication of truth.

Peter Wagner illustrates this when he records an experience from a book written by Raphael Gasson, a former spiritualist medium. "On one occasion during the war years, for example, a man brought Gasson an article belonging to his son who was in the service in order to find out where his son was. Through his spirit 'guide' (it happened to be the spirit of an African witch doctor) Gasson found out that the owner of the article was well and a prisoner of war. The father then proceeded to show Gasson a telegram from the war department stating that his son had been killed in action over two weeks previously. Gasson went back to his guide and verified that the soldier really was not dead and that the father would have this confirmed in three days. Sure enough, three days later the father got a telegram from the war department apologizing for the mistake and saying that the boy was well and a prisoner of war." [1]

Although Satan does not have the ability to read the future, he can give apparent prophecies and then work to make them come true. The fulfillment of most of these false prophecies is turned aside by the protecting hand of God over His people and the affairs of nations. Satan can afflict people with various pains and physical disorders and then work apparent miracles as he removes his satanic power from them. Although Satan cannot work real miracles of healing (because he does not have creative power), his counterfeits will be so realistic that even God's very elect will be deceived, if that is possible (Matthew 24:24). A so-called faith healer conducted mass healing services. People threw their crutches away, walked out of wheelchairs, apparently received sight and hearing. He also preached that Christians today no longer need to observe the Ten Commandments. "We are free in Jesus" was his slogan. Unfortunately, this man was eventually deported from the country for fraud and immorality. As Jesus said "You will know them by their fruits" (Matthew 7:16).

Wonderful Weapons

To be successful in the warfare internal and external, we must have the right weapons. Let me tell you about the weapons that have helped me. You may have known others, but at least you can be sure of not missing one of these vital success armaments. "For the weapons of our warfare are not carnal but mighty in God for pulling down strongholds" (2 Corinthians 10:4). With these spiritual weapons that God gives, you can pull down the strongholds of Satan. Please become extremely skilled in the use of these weapons. Your spiritual survival depends on it. God expects us to combine our human effort with His power in defeating the enemy.

The first weapon is complete confidence in the inner presence of the Holy Spirit. As he talks of evil spirits John confirms our first weapon against them. "You are of God, little children, and have overcome them, because He who is in you is greater than he who is in the world" (1 John 4:4). The Holy Spirit who dwells within us is all-powerful. "That He would grant you, according to the riches of His glory, to be strengthened with might through His Spirit in the inner man" (Ephesians 3:16). The world, the flesh, and the devil cannot be victorious in the face of the Holy Spirit's conscious presence in your life. Notice that Paul continues to say that through the Holy Spirit Jesus Christ dwells in our hearts by faith (verse 17).

By the blood of Jesus we are cleansed from all sin. This is the way the inner witness of the Spirit leads us to overcome by the blood of the Lamb

(Revelation 12:11). Jesus could say, "The ruler of this world is coming, and he has nothing in Me" (John 14:30). When you are convicted by the Holy Spirit that you are completely forgiven and cleansed through the blood of Jesus, then Satan can have no claim on you. You can confidently assert, "Greater is He that is in me than he that is in the world." And in that battle of inner or outer warfare you will be completely successful.

George had lived in failure most of his life. Finally he became addicted to gambling and eventually lost all that he had, including his self-respect. George was brought by a friend to an evangelistic meeting, and there as I explained the gospel from the Word of God, George gave his life to Jesus and was eventually baptized into the family of God. But the big question remained: Could George resist the powerful inner urge to gamble? The devil—miraculously, it seemed—provided tickets to gambling events. "I burned them," George said, shaking his head in amazement. "How did I get the strength to do that?" George really knew the answer, for greater was He that was in George than he that was in the world. "You've done so much evil and made such a mess of your life, George—you are not worth anything. You are just a fraud. Enjoy yourself. A little more evil won't hurt you. Just think about it even if you don't do it." As these thoughts circulated in George's mind many times, he had the answer, which was a spiritual victory weapon. "The blood of Jesus, I claim the blood of Jesus right now. I am forgiven. I am a child of God. Greater is He that is in me than he that is in the world." As I review some of my own sad defeats at the hand of the evil one, I realize now that I had for a time lost the awareness of the Holy Spirit and the love of Jesus within me. I do not want to make that mistake again, because I have tasted the joy of victory in Jesus.

Let me tell you about another weapon that has helped me greatly. I have often quoted Romans 8:28: "And we know that all things work together for good to those who love God, to those who are the called according to His purpose." If all things work together for good, that sounds like victory to me. But notice the secret in the preceding verses: "Likewise the Spirit also helps in our weaknesses. For we do not know what we should pray for as we ought, but the Spirit Himself makes intercession for us with groanings which cannot be uttered. Now He who searches the heart knows what the mind of the Spirit is, because He makes intercession for the saints according to the will of God" (verses 26, 27). The Holy Spirit works on the heart and mind of those He fills, bringing out deeply sincere and fervent prayers that indicate a complete submission to the will of God. This is sometimes called "praying in the Spirit" (Jude 20; 1 Corinthians 14:15).

After Paul has spoken in Ephesians 6 of the conflict and the essential armor, he again turns his attention and ours to praying in the Spirit. "Praying always with all prayer and supplication in the Spirit, being watchful to this end with all perseverance and supplication for all the saints" (verse 18). Professor Clinton E. Arnold, who has written on the conflict between God's people and evil in Ephesians, has said, "If Paul were to summarize the primary way of gaining access to the power of God for waging successful spiritual warfare, he would unwaveringly affirm that it was prayer. Paul models this activity in his two prayers recorded in Ephesians 1 and 3. In essence, Paul prays that God would endow his readers with power so that they could successfully resist the temptations of Satan and be divinely enabled to proclaim the gospel fearlessly in spite of demonic hostility." [2]

Personal prayer that is powerful against the devil within us and in the world around us will involve quality time in communion with God. Praying in the Holy Spirit over the past four years has led me into two forms of prayer that are as old as Christianity itself. Many Christians today are discovering great help in praying through the Lord's Prayer. This has changed my life. So let me summarize briefly the way I move through this prayer each day.

1. Become aware of God's presence. "Our Father in heaven." Through the Holy Spirit heaven is near and God's presence is within us. He is Yahweh shammah—the Lord who is present. It is important to be aware of God's presence right through the day.

2. Praise the name of God. There are 14 names of God that I meditate on each day (Malachi 3:16). Praise God for each of these wonderful aspects of His character represented by His name. The enemy cannot stand in the presence of praise to God's holy name. Your praise drives back the power of Satan. [3] Never miss an opportunity to praise God. This is one of your mighty weapons.

3. Now come into complete surrender to God. "Your will be done." Put yourself and those on your special prayer list right into the hands of God. This is how the Holy Spirit intercedes for us according to God's will. God works out His will within us as we are willing to serve Him. Nothing took the pressure of facing a new day off me more than this. I can face each day in the will of God and not be dominated by my own foolish choices.

4. Every need can be brought before God. He will "give us . . . our daily bread" physically and spiritually. In a time of great need He miraculously provided a house for our family. Not only were we able to get clothes we needed, but our garden grew enough to share with friends and neighbors.

5. Awareness of forgiveness and assurance of salvation through the blood of Jesus is, as we have already noticed, an essential weapon against evil. "Forgive us our sins, for we also forgive everyone who is indebted to us" (Luke 11:4). A forgiving spirit also works wonders for personal victory.

6. Of course, we ask for absolute protection from evil and deliverance from the forces of darkness. He is Yahweh-nissi, our banner of victory. Claim this protection. Believe in this protection. God does not fail.

7. The prayer ends by praising God again. "For Yours is the kingdom and the power and the glory." In this daily prayer there is a double emphasis on praise, because praise is one of your most powerful weapons. Never miss an opportunity to praise God publicly.

The other method of prayer that has given Christians great strength is praying through the Scriptures. George Mueller, the great man of faith, followed this method of spiritual fortification. Sometimes I have taken the Bible and prayed right through it verse by verse over a period of one year. In this way Scripture begins to live in my mind and heart. Promises are readily recalled and deception can be clearly discerned in relationship to the Word of truth. I have also prayed many times through all of the Bible references to the Holy Spirit. You will find them listed at the end of this book.

Notice how Paul spoke of the Scriptures as he addressed spiritual warfare: "And take the helmet of salvation, and the sword of the Spirit, which is the Word of God" (Ephesians 6:17). With the sword of Scripture you can take an offensive stance against evil within or without. The enemy can be defeated. This refers not to defeating people but to vanquishing the lusts of the flesh and the external forces of Satan.

Jesus says that when the strong man is bound, his goods can be plundered. You can pray that Satan will be bound and that the goods of your life (or other people's lives) he is holding will be released. This gives God permission to act against Satan. Now, as God says, "even the captives of the mighty shall be taken away, and the prey of the terrible be delivered; for I will contend with him who contends with you, and I will save your children" (Isaiah 49:25). What a promise! God says, "I will fight for you." By claiming the promises of God's Word, you can use the sword of the Spirit to limit the power of evil forces effectively.

Now, here is another method of victory. Though a born-again Spirit-filled Christian is never alone, there is tremendous extra strength in people praying together. This is why the Holy Spirit leads us into the body of Christ. We are baptized into that body (1 Corinthians 12:13), and that body is the church (Ephesians 1:22, 23). This body draws together in love and can edify or build up those who are part of the church family (Ephesians 4:16). Because of this strength, Jesus clearly stated that the gates of hell would not prevail against His church (Matthew 16:18).

This emphasis on the body is essential, because you cannot survive easily alone in the battle against evil. Let me give a couple illustrations of how the New Testament believers found in church fellowship a weapon of great strength against evil. Remember that in the time of the New Testament the word "church" referred to people—small groups of people meeting primarily in houses in the communities and neighborhoods in which they worked; people who studied, prayed, and shared together. When Peter and John were severely threatened, they came to their companions for combined prayer (Acts 4:23-31). The strength that resulted from this meeting shook the world. Paul earnestly desired to come to the house churches in Rome, and his reason is clear: "Now I beg you, brethren, through the Lord Jesus Christ, and through the love of the Spirit, that you strive together with me in your prayers to God for me" (Romans 15:30).

Do you have a small group of praying friends who will pray at least weekly with you and daily for you? Have you given them a Bible promise to claim for you? The people who pray for me have given me incredible strength in the Lord as I have ministered in many parts of the world. I sat on a platform in Brazil with 1,600 people waiting for me to speak. The old enemy seemed to say, "You are too tired and sick. Get someone else to speak, or send the people home." Suddenly I remembered that Don Jacobsen was praying for me. That my wife, Barbara, was praying for me. That my children were praying for me. I could think of a dozen people whom I knew were upholding me in prayer. Suddenly I felt a strength enter my body and a clarity in my mind. As a result, God used me to speak in a way that brought more than 1,000 decisions for ministry in the name of Jesus.

A pastor struggled with an addiction to TV that had subtly crept upon him. When he shared this problem with his small group, they prayed earnestly for him. They prayed in the Spirit, presenting the pastor before God and fervently asking that he be fully open to God's will. They also pledged to pray for the pastor early each day. No wonder that pastor got the victory! A ministry that was severely threatened by Satan was saved.

Recently I listened to another pastor, Chad McComas, tell of the tremendous strength he has gained from the 15 people who meet regularly to pray for him and his wife, Debbie. "We usually gather on Friday evening," Chad explained at a meeting of fellow pastors. "The group pray from 9:00 p.m. until midnight, and then they covenant to intercede for us each day as we serve God. The Lord has given me great strength from this. It has revolutionized my ministry."

You too can discern and defeat the enemy by the use of your spiritual weapons. Put on the whole armor of God. Resist the devil, and he will flee from you. He is a defeated foe. You are a victorious Christian because greater is He that is in you than he that is in the world. In this world you will have tribulation, but because you have, by the Holy Spirit, the Prince of Peace, you will have peace, and that peace will be beyond the understanding of the world around you.

Discerning and Defeating the Enemy

Cohesive Contrasts

A group should give spiritual support, not cheap advice, to those with problems. A group member in serious trouble should be directed by the leader to competent and professional advisors who can be used of God to help solve the crisis.

Do you have an experience you would like to share telling of strength you have received from strong spiritual support by others? Perhaps you faced loss of job, failure at school, death of a loved one, family crisis, health problems, etc.

Consideration of the Word
Study Text: Ephesians 6:10-16

How would you define the "wiles of the devil" (Ephesians 6:11)? _____

_____

_____

The Bible talks of internal and external conflict as a result of evil. The internal conflict comes from our old sinful nature (Romans 7:23, 24). The external conflict often comes from Satan himself (1 Peter 5:8). Which area of conflict do you find easiest to deal with? Why is this? _____

_____

Paul seems to indicate that we face a rather formidable foe (Ephesians 6:12). From this chapter, what do you see as some of the most dangerous tricks and counterfeits Satan will work? _____

The only way to discern deceptions is to compare them with Bible truth. List some ways the Bible, with the Ten Commandments and words of Jesus, will enable us to test the spirits (Isaiah 8:20; 1 John 4:1). _____

If you saw an apparent miracle right now, what would your reaction be?

Follow the miracle worker _____ Check the facts _____ Wait to see the fruitage _____ Praise God _____ Believe it by faith _____ Look for repentance and deep commitment to God and His truth _____ Other _____

Paul says to put on the whole armor of God. This includes offensive and defensive weapons that will break down strongholds (2 Corinthians 10:4). Why do you think that the certainty of the indwelling presence of the Holy Spirit is so important (1 John 4:4)? _____

How much can Satan claim within us if we are sure that our sins are forgiven by the blood of Jesus? _____

Can you give an example of the powerful weapon that praying always in the Spirit (Ephesians 6:18) has been or could have been for you? _____

We can pray that Satan will be bound (Matthew 12:29) and his captives taken away (Isaiah 49:25). What a promise! Are there some captives you would like to see set free right now? Who or what are they? _____

_____

_____

New Testament leaders such as Jesus, Peter, John, and Paul depended heavily on a small group of praying friends and also a larger church group of intercessors. Does this seem strange to you? Can you suggest an important reason for this united effort? _____

_____

Conversation With the Lord

First, praise God for victory through "the power of His might." Thank Him that "He who is in you is greater than he who is in the world." Sing some songs of victory in Jesus.

Second, pray for specific needs and conflicts group members or others are facing.

Close by praying through the seven sections of the Lord's Prayer.

Committing the Word to Memory

This week, write out Ephesians 6:17, 18. Memorize these verses, then share them with someone as soon as possible.

_____

_____

_____

CHAPTER ELEVEN

The Leading Question

No Animals," the sign said on the entrance door to a large shopping center. I had noticed this sign many times, so was surprised to see a dog making its way through the crowded concourse on the lower level. It was quickly obvious, however, that this was no ordinary animal. A lady whose eyes appeared totally sightless gripped the special handle attached to her seeing-eye dog, and with remarkable confidence they both moved rapidly through the crowd to some prearranged destination.

Led by a dog! What am I led by today? In a spiritual sense, whatever leads us indicates to whom or what we belong. Although the lady in the shopping center certainly did not belong to the dog, the dog was an indication that she belonged to the world of the blind. The Bible clearly illustrates this principle as it discusses the role of the Holy Spirit in your life and mine. "For as many as are led by the Spirit of God, these are sons of God" (Romans 8:14). Jesus used some rather humorous visual imagery to picture the risk of being led by sightless substitutes of the Holy Spirit. "And if the blind leads the blind, both will fall into a ditch" (Matthew 15:14). The children of God stay out of the ditch because their Guide knows the way of joy and peace.

In the songs of the Jewish people there was, in Bible times, a consciousness of the absolute necessity of God's direct leading of His children. "Lead me, O Lord, in Your righteousness" (Psalm 5:8). "Lead me in Your truth" (Psalm 25:5). "Lead me in a smooth path" (Psalm 27:11). "Lead me to the rock that is higher than I" (Psalm 61:2). How did David see this leading take place? In Psalm 139, after speaking of the omnipresence of the Holy Spirit, he said, "Even there Your hand shall lead me, and Your right hand shall hold me" (verse 10). If you have a guide who can be everywhere and has all power, you can have complete trust, because you have placed your hand into the hand of God.

"Hold my hand." How often mothers and fathers say this to their little children, especially in the face of possible confusion or danger. God says, "Hold My hand, and I will lead you along into the path of righteousness." To allow God to lead us is an act of complete dependence on Him. We willingly give Him our will, because we know that He will never lead us other than we ourselves would choose to be led if we knew the end from the beginning. Willingness to submit to God's leading is possible only if we have been born again by the Spirit and are a part of God's family. "For as many as are led by the Spirit of God, these are the sons of God" (Romans 8:14). What a family! This family knows who they are and where they are going. "Jesus answered, 'Most assuredly, I say to you, unless one is born of water and the Spirit, he cannot enter the kingdom of God. That which is born of the flesh is flesh, and that which is born of the Spirit is spirit. Do not marvel that I said to you, "You must be born again" ' " (John 3:5-7).

On the front of a bus you can usually read the destination. If you are traveling by the Spirit with the family of God, your destination is the kingdom of heaven. It is important to be on the right bus heading for the right destination.

Who Is Leading?

Let us think for a moment of the way our family connection is indicated by whatever we allow to lead us. For instance, I can enjoy some recreational sports and even benefit physically from them, but if my life is led by that sport, then my direction will be away from the kingdom of God. While I need to be dressed cleanly, neatly, and even attractively according to the culture in which I live, yet if my life is dominated by fashion and expensive externals, it is possible that I am gripping the hand of another god. I am on a bus going to the wrong destination. Now, this can get a little personal, but you and I both know that there are dozens of gods that can lead us to break our family connection. If people have not yet made a commitment to Jesus, these blind guides will lead them away from prayerfully considering new birth into the family of God. Think of what can happen with music, eating and drinking, houses or land, etc., if they become gods. They push people onto the wrong bus, and often the destination is disaster.

Here is a test that has really helped me. In a quiet place away from all distractions I pause, reach out my hand, and ask, trying to be completely honest with myself, "Who or what is leading me? Who or what is holding this hand and determining the direction of my life?" I found in that wonderful little book *Steps to Christ* some questions that are very searching. "Who has the heart? With whom are our thoughts? Of whom do we love to converse? Who has our warmest affections and our best energies?[1] Please take a moment to ask yourself those questions right now. Of course, you may already know the answer, but are you willing to admit it to yourself and God? I have struggled here a number of times, but I am glad that the Holy Spirit gives us strength to change leaders and allow God to really guide our lives. On one occasion at a small group house meeting where we were studying *Steps to Christ* I first came across the statement that we just read from page 58. Without even pausing, I knew the answer. The Holy Spirit had convicted me that I was not being led by the Lord I represented as a pastor. It was hard; it hurt. I did not want to admit it, but the surrender of that problem of selfishness to God helped save my ministry.

If only Angelo had taken time to ask honestly and sincerely who or what was leading him. Angelo did not just drive cars, they drove him as he made a decision to be a part of the car god family. Angelo's taste for expensive cars led him to work at two jobs. As an electrician his earnings were high, and eventually his dream came true. For his honeymoon Angelo bought a brand-new bright-red Ferrari. It was a fabulous piece of engineering and a beauty to behold. Just before the wedding Angelo changed the tires on his new car so it would be perfect for the long fast drive across the state. But the car god led Angelo into tragedy. At 100 miles per hour a front tire blew, and in a moment Angelo and his new bride were dead in the wreckage of their car. Tragedy does not often come that quickly, but the eternal consequences of being led by any false god will eventually become painfully clear.

Led in Ministry

Where does the Holy Spirit lead us? Certainly not into temptation (Matthew 6:13). Like the Good Shepherd, He leads us in the paths of righteousness (Psalm 23:2). And especially He guides us into all truth (John 16:13). Principally, though, the Holy Spirit is given in His wholeness and completeness to lead God's children so they can share in ministry for their heavenly Father. It is incredible to see the direct leading of the Holy Spirit in the ministry of the disciples in the book of Acts. For instance, the Spirit led Philip to join the Ethiopian official on his chariot (Acts 8:29). Paul and Barnabas were led to Seleucia and Cyprus (Acts

13:4). On the other hand, the Spirit closed the door to Bithynia (Acts 16:7).

It is exciting to be led as directly as the servants of God in Acts. God is still doing it today, as lives are surrendered to Him. Recently Attorney Herald Follett told me of some of the amazing ways the Spirit has led in his life. Even through the tragic death of his daughter, Kari, Herald sees the hand of God leading him into a very fruitful television ministry. Dr. Kurt Johnson tells of the Spirit's leading, which, quite unexpectedly, brought him to the place where he could write a very helpful book on small group ministries. Without previous anticipation Robert Folkenberg was elected as world president of my denomination. Even though they had prayed earnestly, those who participated in the election expressed surprise at the direct leading of God. Interestingly, when one looks back on Pastor Folkenberg's life and ministry, it is possible to see the Spirit leading in many different ways in preparation for this tremendous task.

Perhaps the most comprehensive illustration of the Spirit's leading is seen in the experience of Peter and Cornelius as recorded in Acts 10. You will remember that Peter had a weird vision of all sorts of strange creatures lowered from heaven in a sheet (verses 9-16). Obviously Peter thought and prayed a great deal about this vision. I know I would have. Suddenly the Spirit spoke directly to Peter, informing him that three men were seeking him (verse 19). I would certainly like to be so closely in tune with the Holy Spirit that I could hear His voice.

But it was not only Peter who had been given a vision. So had a Gentile Roman centurion, Cornelius. Although he had been praying to God and making large donations to religious charities, Cornelius was considered unacceptable for Peter's association because of racial and religious prejudice. Peter would not have responded to the three men that Cornelius sent to his door if it had not been for the strange vision he was given of the unclean creatures in the sheet.

Because of the direct leading of the Holy Spirit Peter accepted the invitation to the house meeting in Caesarea. The Spirit told him to go, "doubting nothing" (Acts 11:12). Six men traveled with Peter, and eventually they found themselves in the large house of Cornelius, where many people had gathered (Acts 10:24, 27).

Now Peter revealed that God had shown him the meaning of his vision. "Then he said to them, 'You know how unlawful it is for a Jewish man to keep company with or go to one of another nation. But God has shown me that I should not call any man common or unclean' " (verse

28). It is possible to miss opportunities to share the love of Jesus and exercise the spiritual gifts He has given us because we consider people around us radically different from ourselves. Even although they may be of different races, colors, religions, standards, morals, education or socioeconomic status than we are, the Holy Spirit leads us to call no person "common or unclean."

I have spoken a number of times in a church in Jerusalem where Jews and Palestinians worshiped together. I have worshiped in a church in Seoul with Koreans and Japanese praising God together. I have seen Blacks and Whites embracing as brothers and sisters in Jesus. I guess that you can list numerous illustrations of walls of prejudice and teaching that can be broken down only by the love of Jesus (Ephesians 2:15; Galatians 3:28). Does this mean that the Holy Spirit makes us all the same? No. There will always be important differences between the sexes, races, and cultures, and we can praise God for that, but led by the Spirit, we are united as one in Jesus.

Cornelius in Acts 10 explains to the group the significance of his vision. One part of this especially surprised me, although I should have expected it—God gave Cornelius Peter's exact address. "Send therefore to Joppa and call Simon here, whose surname is Peter. He is lodging in the house of Simon, a tanner, by the sea. When he comes, he will speak to you" (Acts 10:32). I wonder how many people God has given my address and yet when the Holy Spirit has led them to my door at home, school, or work I did not recognize them as opportunities God had given me to witness for Him. Perhaps I have considered these people so unlike me that I did not even give them a second thought.

In this first house-church in Caesarea Peter is led by the Spirit to exalt Jesus. That is the ministry of the Spirit and Spirit-led people (John 16:14). So Peter boldly announces that Jesus is "Lord of all" (Acts 10:36). Peter in his group discussion then explains the amazing power behind the ministry of Jesus. "How God anointed Jesus of Nazareth with the Holy Spirit and with power, who went about doing good and healing all who were oppressed by the devil, for God was with him" (verse 38). This brief condensation of Peter's study climaxes with the great gospel invitation as the prevenient grace of God worked on the hearts of these Gentile people. "To Him all the prophets witness that, through His name, whoever believes in Him will receive remission of sins" (verse 43).

The results of belief in the house of Cornelius are dramatic. The exclusiveness and limitations of Jewish Christianity were overthrown forever. Like a grenade bursting in a glass house, all preconceived ideas and prejudices were shattered by the outpouring of the Holy Spirit. And to confound things still more, it happened even before water baptism. "While Peter was still speaking these words, the Holy Spirit fell upon all those who heard the word. And those of the circumcision who believed were astonished, as many as came with Peter, because the gift of the Holy Spirit had been poured out on the Gentiles also. For they heard them speak with tongues and magnify God. Then Peter answered, 'Can anyone forbid water, that these should not be baptized who have received the Holy Spirit just as we have?' And he commanded them to be baptized in the name of the Lord. Then they asked him to stay a few days" (verses 44-48).

I can imagine the astonishment of the six Christians who came with Peter, but it was exceeded by the amazement of the church leaders at the Jerusalem headquarters. They were speechless. "When they heard these things they became silent; and they glorified God, saying, 'Then God has also granted to the Gentiles repentance to life' " (Acts 11:18). Have you ever felt that way? Have you ever felt speechless when you heard of someone who unexpectedly has been filled with the Spirit? Then like the disciples you glorify and praise God for another mighty miracle of His grace.

Recently a pastor told me the miraculous story of his conversion and subsequent filling with the Holy Spirit. He had been brought up in a denomination that had seemed to him to major in uncontrolled emotionalism. As a young person he turned his back on God and joined a wild motorcycle gang. "I was a criminal," he told me with a tone of regret in his voice. "I was into drugs and fighting and reached the lowest level possible." Ten years ago the Holy Spirit led Larry Welch into a Bible study with an enthusiastic Christian, and the miracle of transformation took place. The Lord has used Larry to lead many others to know and accept Jesus as their Saviour. "I want a Spirit-filled ministry every day. I want the freedom to be led by the Holy Spirit," Larry concluded just before praying a beautiful prayer thanking God for the safe journey we had enjoyed together.

Tripping Over Tongues

Out of the experience of Peter and Cornelius a very common question arises. I saw this illustrated a number of times as I was speaking about the Holy Spirit on a live television program during which viewers could call in questions on the topic. As the phones began to ring, this question came from places as far apart as Texas, Michigan, and California. "What about tongues? Is this the sign or evidence of the filling and the leading of the Holy Spirit?" Christians in modern times have been greatly divided over the gift of tongues. Some say it is the gift of ability to speak in a foreign language for the spreading of the gospel. Others have said that in the light of 1 Corinthians 14, tongues are the language of heaven. I could quote numerous respected authorities on both views, as there are many sincere Christian scholars who have written on this subject.

It was obvious, though, that in the experience of Peter and Cornelius, tongues were considered a sign. Without a doubt the people of Caesarea had received the filling of the Holy Spirit, because this was immediately obvious by the gift of tongues that they were given. "And as I began to speak, the Holy Spirit fell upon them, as upon us at the beginning" (Acts 11:15). Clearly the tongues at Caesarea were the same as the languages at Pentecost. You will remember from reading in Acts 2 that people from at least 14 language groups exclaimed, "And how is it that we hear, each in our own language in which we were born?" (Acts 2:8).

Let me give you some of my own conclusions on tongues. You may not agree with me, but at least we can explore this together and pray for love and light from the Spirit of God. In this matter I also want to be led by the Spirit, because I am a child of God and I want to follow in His way and certainly be led into all truth.

First, it is likely that there is a language of heaven. Most of us think of God speaking our own language, and I am sure He can, but what the language of heaven is we do not know. Some believe it is Spanish, and I am not going to argue with that. Paul says, "Though I speak with the tongues of men and of angels . . ." (1 Corinthians 13:1). So perhaps the angels do use the language of heaven, but I am not convinced that this is actually what Paul is saying here.

Nowhere do I find that the gift of tongues is given to all Christians. "But one and the same Spirit works all these things, distributing to each one individually as He wills. . . . Are all apostles? Are all prophets? Are all teachers? Are all workers of miracles? Do all have gifts of healings? Do all speak with tongues? Do all interpret?" (1 Corinthians 12:11-30). Paul obviously makes it clear that not all Christians, even in his time, had the gift of tongues. In view of this, I find it hard to imagine that God would give the language of heaven (if that is what it is) to a few select Christians. In fact, Paul clearly states that tongues are a sign, not for believers so they can have a private prayer language, but for unbelievers so they can hear the gospel (1 Corinthians 14:22).

Second, it appears that no gift is given for the personal benefit of a believer, but rather for witness, outreach, or the organization and growth of the body of believers, the church. All the gifts that Paul lists in Romans 12 are for the one purpose of helping others. The same applies to Ephesians 4. In 1 Corinthians 14 it appears that the missionary gift of languages was being misused. People with tongues were speaking in groups where no one understood. Apparently the speakers did not understand themselves, yet they did get some personal benefit from speaking in tongues knowing that they were exercising their gift (verses 1-4). No one else was helped by these tongues unless there was an interpreter present. If this situation developed today with the true gift of tongues, then I believe it would be best for the unity and orderliness of the church if that gift were exercised only for missionary outreach or privately at home.

Third, I asked former tongues-speaking pastor, Rick Odle, graduate of two Bible colleges, why he turned away from tongues as the infallible initial sign of the baptism of the Holy Spirit. His reply was very interesting. "I have seen tongues in many cases that were artificially contrived or manufactured with high-pressure emotionalism. I also observed that many of my parishioners who spoke in tongues never once witnessed about Jesus to their neighbors or associates. The desire to spread the truth of Jesus' Word just did not seem to exist. I studied the subject of tongues with thoroughness and earnest prayer and saw no support for the belief that this one gift is the sign of the Spirit's power." Rick himself is a Spirit-filled Christian, a Spirit-led child of God full of the love of Jesus. Today his ministry centers on leading people to Jesus, leading them to know the great truths of the Bible and showing how they can know victory power by the filling of the Holy Spirit.

Where Does He Lead?

Sometimes when we are led by the Spirit we pass through a valley before the high point of rejoicing. Sometimes there are many valleys. David, as he wrote of God's marvelous leading, also spoke of the valley. "Though I walk through the valley of the shadow of death I will fear no evil" (Psalm 23:4). At the first pastors' Holy Spirit Fellowship that was organized in Oregon our song leaders were evangelist Paul Johnson and his wife, Corleen. Corleen was excited about learning more of the Holy Spirit, but soon a darkness seemed to settle over her, and eventually that night she walked around the grounds of the retreat center in tears, crying for some hope, some ray of light. "I seemed to feel that it was my sin that was cutting me off from the presence of the Holy Spirit," Corleen later testified to the group. "Yet I could not bring a specific sin to mind." Paul and others prayed with Corleen and shared promises with her, but it was as if the darkness was locked in place. "Then the Holy Spirit brought something specific to my mind," Corleen continued. "I remembered what happened when my first husband was killed in a plane crash years ago. I had claimed a promise that he was still alive, and as searchers looked for the plane, I firmly believed that everything would be all right. When his body was found five days later, it seemed that inside me there came a distrust of God's promises that has lingered through the years. I also feared to claim a Bible promise, thinking I may be completely let down again." Corleen went on to tell those present how that night she put her distrust and fear into the hands of God for the first time in 21 years. "It was like a tremendous relief came over me. Suddenly I knew that the Spirit had been leading me all the time." Now Corleen sings with greater joy and beauty than ever before. Many people have been tremendously blessed by her testimony and the song that tells the story of the Spirit's leading even through the valley of the shadow of death.

How far does the Spirit lead the children of God? The answer is not hard to find. The Spirit leads God's children home. In fact, the Holy Spirit puts into the hearts of all people that He fills an earnest desire for home. One songwriter has said it this way: "I'm homesick for heaven; seems I cannot wait."

"For we through the Spirit eagerly wait for the hope of righteousness by faith" (Galatians 5:5). Paul understood the Spirit-inspired homesickness of God's children to be with their heavenly Father. What is the hope of righteousness by faith? This is clearly not talking about Spirit-filled people hoping for righteousness. This they already have in Jesus. It is talking of the hope that righteousness by faith brings. A young preacher, E. J. Waggoner, summed it up this way: "If, instead of thinking ourselves so powerful that *we* can do the law, we will allow the Holy Spirit to come in that we may be filled with the righteousness of the law, we will have living hope dwelling in us. The hope of the Spirit—the hope of righteousness by faith—has no element of uncertainty in it. It is positive assurance. In nothing else is there any hope. He who does not have 'the righteousness which is of God by faith' has no hope whatsoever. Only Christ in us is 'the hope of glory.' " [2]

PRAISE GOD FOR THE SPIRIT

GARRIE F. WILLIAMS

CORLEEN JOHNSON

I prayed for the Spir - it, But all that seemed to come Was a sense of sin and guilt - i - ness, That black - ened out my sun. I wan - dered in the dark - ness Hour __ af - ter hour; Had Je - sus for - sak - en me When I had sought his power? __

__ Praise God, the Spir - it healed my wound - ed brok - en heart; Praise God, I have new life in Him. __ I'm walk - ing in His

power, I'm re-joic-ing in His love; Je-sus' Spir-it gives me vic-to-ry,

Fine

vic-to-ry, vic-to-ry!_____ Je-sus' Spir-it gives me vict'-ry o-ver sin.

In the depth of my de-spair The Spir-it spoke to me. Prom-is-es from

Scrip-ture Were used to set me free. The Spir-it brought the light— Beau-ti-ful and

D.S. al Fine

clear; Je-sus' love with-in me Re-placed my doubt and fear. Praise

139

So what is this hope of glory? Paul has also spoken of it in Romans. "And not only they, but we also who have the firstfruits of the Spirit, even we ourselves groan within ourselves, eagerly waiting for the adoption, the redemption of our body" (Romans 8:23). At conversion we receive the down payment of the Holy Spirit, which is an earnest or guarantee of what God finally has in store for His children (Ephesians 1:14; 4:30; 1 Corinthians 1:22; 5:5). These are the firstfruits of the Spirit.

When is the day of redemption? When is the redemption of the body? Without a doubt the Bible clearly points to the second coming of Jesus as the great moment when, at the resurrection, all of God's children's hopes will be fulfilled. "For the Lord Himself will descend from heaven with a shout, with the voice of an archangel, and with the trumpet of God. And the dead in Christ will rise first. Then we who are alive and remain shall be caught up together with them in the clouds to meet the Lord in the air. And thus we shall always be with the Lord" (1 Thessalonians 4:16, 17).

I have an old Bible commentary written during the past century by Anglican bishop Christopher Wordsworth. Wordsworth was a nephew of the famous English poet. He had been a brilliant scholar in classics and mathematics at Cambridge and while headmaster at Harrow felt called to serve the Lord in a special way. He began his commentary on the Bible in 1856 and concluded it just after he became bishop of Lincoln. Notice what he says concerning the hope in Galatians 5:5. "For we, by the operation of the Holy Ghost, look forth from faith, as our foundation, and wait for the blessed hope (Titus 2:13), the hope laid up in heaven (Colossians 1:5), as the fruit and reward of the justification first conveyed to us when we put on Christ . . . and which receives fresh occasions of sanctification by the daily renewing of the Holy Ghost (Titus 3:5), and which is consummated in the 'new heavens and new earth wherein dwelleth righteousness' (2 Peter 3:13, KJV)."[3]

As Wordsworth says, the hope of righteousness by faith is called also by Paul the blessed hope and glorious appearing of our great God and Saviour Jesus Christ (Titus 2:13). Without a doubt those who are led by the Spirit will have the hope of the return of Jesus burning in their hearts. When an individual or church group lose their earnestness for the Second Coming and resurrection, it is an indication that the Holy Spirit has not been given complete access to their lives.

Here is the question: Who or what is leading you today? Are you heading for home with the family? "For as many as are led by the Spirit of God, these are sons of God" (Romans 8:14).

SMALL GROUP STUDY

The Leading Question

Cohesive Contrasts

In an earlier study guide, reference was made to the first two seasons in the experience of most groups—"honeymoon" and "disillusionment." The third season is "synthesis." Even though new members join the group, there is a strong sense of cohesion, as contrasting values, strengths, and gifts of group members are united in achieving original and new goals.

Here is an interesting question to begin the group meeting: In what particular role that I find myself is it easiest for me to be a real person? For example, student, parent, son or daughter, employee, employer, neighbor, group member, etc. Why?

Consideration of the Word
Study Text: Acts 10:17-48

Whom do you most easily identify with in the story in Acts 10? Why?

Peter _____ Cornelius _____ The angel _____

Peter's companions _____ Cornelius' three men _____

The friends and relatives of Cornelius _____ The leaders in Jerusalem _____

Other _____

How willing are you to be led? Give a reason for your answer. _____

_____

_____

Paul said that God's children are led by the Holy Spirit (Romans 8:14). How would you define the Spirit's leading? _____

_____

_____

_____

What test questions do you find most effective to determine who or what is leading you in the major emphasis of your life? _____

_____

_____

_____

Primarily the Holy Spirit leads into ministry. How is this illustrated by Peter's experience with Cornelius (Acts 10:19)? _____

_____

_____

_____

What are some ways prejudice can hinder a Christian from following the Holy Spirit's leading (verse 28)? _____

_____

_____

God gave Cornelius Peter's exact address. What surprises you and what challenges you about this? _____

_____

_____

The Holy Spirit was poured out on the people at the small group meeting in the house of Cornelius. They immediately received the gift of tongues (verse 45). In what way do you see this as a sign (Acts 11:15, 17)? _____

_____

Apparently all the gifts are for witness and ministry, not private edification. Can you find evidence in 1 Corinthians 12 that the gift of tongues is not given to all Spirit-filled Christians? _____

_____

_____

Here is an interesting exercise. List all the reasons you can think of that the Holy Spirit would create in a believer an earnest desire for the return of Jesus (Galatians 5:5). Which of these reasons do you find most motivational? _____

_____

Paul calls the return of Jesus the blessed hope (Titus 2:13), and Christians overflow with hope by the Holy Spirit (Romans 15:13). How can this sort of hope be a contagious leading factor in a hope-less world? _____

_____

_____

Conversation With the Lord

The Lord has led this group a long way together. There have been many wonderful answers to prayer.

First, praise God for His leading.

Second, put all present in the group into the leading hand of God. Ask that others outside the group will be open to God's leading by the Holy Spirit.

Finally, after praying for specific needs, pray for God's leading in your nation and in areas of world problems. Finish with the Lord's Prayer.

Committing the Word to Memory

This week, write out Acts 10:44, 45. Memorize these verses, then share them with someone as soon as possible.

Hurting or Helping
the Spirit?

Angela and I have been friends for three years, but today at school she wouldn't talk to me." Diane was obviously depressed by this strange action. "I asked her if she wanted help with her homework, but she just said, 'Leave me alone.' "

Peter, a recently baptized Christian, was very enthusiastic about his newfound faith in Jesus. "Don't get so excited," an older church member said with a knowing smile on his face. "You will be as spiritually dead as the rest of us soon." Randy sat watching television most of the day while his college colleagues studied hard for their finals. "I couldn't care less whether I pass or fail," Randy explained to his puzzled friends. "These college courses are worthless anyway. I can get any job I want with the influence of some family friends."

Jessica asked the two ladies who came to study the Bible with her if she could pray for them. "Please don't," they quickly replied. "You would not be praying to the same God as we believe in."

What do these few experiences have in common? Perhaps only one thing. They illustrate some strange ways Christians and non-Christians can treat your friend and mine, the Holy Spirit. "And do not grieve the Holy Spirit of God, by whom you were sealed for the day of redemption" (Ephesians 4:30). "Do not quench the Spirit" (1 Thessalonians 5:19). "You always resist the Holy Spirit" (Acts 7:51). "Therefore I say to you, every sin and blasphemy will be forgiven men, but the blasphemy against the Spirit will not be forgiven men. Anyone who speaks a word against the Son of Man, it will be forgiven him; but whoever speaks against the Holy Spirit, it will not be forgiven him either in this age or in the age to come" (Matthew 12:31, 32).

After studying throughout this book on how to be filled with the Holy Spirit and receive His daily blessings, we must reluctantly consider the possibility of losing or rejecting the Holy Spirit. Unfortunately, this can and does happen.

Now, I want to give you some early warning signals, because people who are progressively closed to the Holy Spirit become less and less concerned about it. They seem to feel that they can make their way in the world quite satisfactorily without any real help from God; that natural abilities and business contacts will see them through. Some also keep enough cultural religion to ease their conscience as far as the possibility of a future life is concerned. Satan's subtlety in gradually separating us from the comfort and strength of the Holy Spirit needs to be unmasked so that we will not be ignorant of his devices (2 Corinthians 2:11).

When I asked a group why it is that we need to be continually filled with the Holy Spirit, one man replied, "Because we leak." Although this explanation sounds a little crude, it does identify an important point of truth. When a crack in the dam is small, leakage can be stopped. When the dam breaks, the flood washes away all hope, and the raging water carries lives and property into oblivion. I want to identify the early warnings of leakage clearly so we can immediately repair the damage through the healing power of Jesus.

Is it really possible to lose the Holy Spirit? David was deeply concerned about this when he prayed, "Do not take Your Holy Spirit from me" (Psalm 51:11). Actually David himself had wandered away from God spiritually, and this had resulted in his terrible sin. Now he realized how far he was from being filled with the Holy Spirit. He had lost the assurance of salvation and longed for this ministry of the Holy Spirit again. "Restore to me the joy of Your salvation, and uphold me with Your generous spirit" (verse 12).

Saul had been changed into another man by the Holy Spirit (1 Samuel 10:6), but eventually Saul's pride and disobedience led to the place where the Spirit of the Lord departed from him (1 Samuel 16:14).

Grieving a Gracious Friend

In view of the experiences of David and Saul we notice Paul's urgent warning. "Do not grieve the Holy Spirit of God, by whom you were sealed for the day of redemption" (Ephesians 4:30). Paul is obviously talking to converted people, because he says that they have been sealed by the Holy Spirit. I was interested in this word "grieve," because it means heaviness of heart. When Jesus was in Gethsemane, He was "sorrowful, even unto death" (Matthew 26:38). "Sorrowful" is translated from the same word as "grieve" and "heaviness." What actions in a converted person's life can cause this hurting of the Holy Spirit?

The Holy Spirit Himself gives us a warning. "Beware, brethren, lest there be in any of you an evil heart of unbelief in departing from the living God; but exhort one another daily while it is called 'Today,' lest any of you be hardened through the deceitfulness of sin" (Hebrews 3:13). How does this hardening and unbelief begin to happen to a Christian? I have to be rather practical here and share what I have observed in my own life and the lives of many others. Many times in Hong Kong street tailors have offered to measure me and fit me for a suit that they said would be made overnight. Satan has tailor-made spiritual distractions fitted for every person from childhood to senior years, but most of them fall into a number of general areas.

For instance, many people's spirituality is affected by hours spent watching television. Nothing has influenced the world so much as the RCA experiment with 150 flickering black-and-white television sets in New York City in 1939. Tony Schwartz, professor of telecommunications at New York University, says that no other product has achieved acceptance as fast as television. Much controversy has been raised about the effects of television on morals and society. On the other hand, evidence has been cited for the educational, informational, and relaxational value of television. There is little doubt, however, that television has led many Christians into materialism and pleasure-seeking while minimizing the evils of sin and selfishness by classing such things as immorality and violence as entertainment. In front of television, not only does time for Bible study and prayer evaporate, but so does the desire to spend time in fellowship with God.

David Wilkerson in *The Cross and the Switchblade* tells how, when he sold his television set, the Lord, through prayer, led him into a ministry that changed the lives of thousands of young people. I am not suggesting that you get rid of your set (although some people have benefited in many ways by doing this), but I do suggest that you spend at least as much time in God's Word and prayer as you do watching television. When I began to do this myself, my taste for television programs and even advertising radically altered. Of course, I am not saying that if you watch no television you need not spend any time studying the Word and praying. Perhaps there are some other temptations for you to beware of as you consider your own spiritual life.

There is very little compatibility between the things of the world and the things of the Spirit. I am talking about the world not as people ("God so loved the world"—John 3:16), or as a place ("the earth is the Lord's and all its fullness, the world and those who dwell therein"—Psalm 24:1), but as a principle. Speaking of the world in this way, John says, "Do not love the world or the things in the world. If anyone loves the world, the love of the Father is not in him. For all that is in the world—the lust of the flesh, the lust of the eyes, and the pride of life—is not of the Father but is of the world. And the world is passing away, and the lust of it; but he who does the will of the Father abides forever" (1 John 2:15-17).

There is much in the entertainment world and even printed material that can lead us in the end to grieve the Spirit and not even be concerned about it. The Presbyterian revival pastor Albert Barnes lists from Scripture six ways the Holy Spirit can be grieved: (1) by open and gross sins, (2) by anger, (3) by licentious thoughts and desires, (4) by ingratitude, (5) by neglect, and (6) by resistance. [1]

The Spirit is saddened not only when He sees our heart hardened by sin, but also when we lower our resistance to sin and sickness by mistreating our bodies. James Stewart, the great preacher of the Church of Scotland and professor of New Testament at the University of Edinburgh, emphasizes this when he writes about the reasons for the leakage of Holy Spirit power in Christians today. Telling of an experience in the life of Dr. Timothy Richard, a pioneer missionary to China, he says, "Dr. Richard had given to an educated, cultured Chinese gentleman a copy of the New Testament, and this gentleman promised to read it. When he met Dr. Richard again he said, 'I have read the New Testament through as I promised.' 'Well,' said the doctor, 'what was the deepest impression made upon your mind in reading the New Testament?' To the missionary's surprise he replied, 'The wonderful truth that the body may be the temple of the Holy Spirit.' Surely that pagan gentleman recognized the gloriousness and mystery of the Christian life. Have you been ignoring the claims of Christ upon your body? Have you been grieving the Holy Spirit through sins in the body? Many believers have a wastage of spiritual power because they have not brought their bodies into subjection to the Holy Spirit. It is often surprising to see so many so-called spiritual believers impair the health of the body which is the instrument of the Lord by overindulgence in eating and drinking." [2]

Another writer put it this way: "God cannot let His Holy Spirit rest upon those who, while they know how they should eat for health, persist in a course that will enfeeble mind and body." [3] When I realized that the only way the Holy Spirit can have access to my life is through my brain cells, I decided to observe the eight laws of good health that have brought vitality to the body and clarity of mind to millions of people. Each of these natural remedies and health principles when used properly and in the right balance can enhance your openness, usefulness, courage, and faith in the power of the Holy Spirit. "Pure air, sunlight, abstemiousness, rest, exercise, proper diet, the use of water, trust in divine power." [4] For instance, while no one is going to earn his or her way to heaven by drinking six glasses of pure water per day, the lack of proper fluids in the body will cause a deterioration to certain organs and a clouding of the mind that will make it difficult to perceive spiritual things and spiritually dangerous situations.

I have also sensed the Holy Spirit grieved at times in my own life when I try to do in my own strength things that can be done only in the strength of Jesus. I was sitting in the basement of the men's dormitory at Andrews University waiting for my laundry to dry when a man walked out of the nearby exercise room and passed me in the corridor. He probably was the most muscular individual I have ever seen. I was speechless as he walked by with muscles as large as settee cushions glistening with some type of body oil. Later when I learned that one of the students was a U.S. champion weight lifter, I guessed that this was the man. I imagined, with a smile, what it would have been like if this ball of muscle had approached me requesting help to lift his laundry basket. Tremendous strength available, but struggling to do the lightest task! Can you imagine that?

For born-again Christians the power of the Holy Spirit is immeasurably great. Listen to this: "Now to Him who is able to do exceedingly abundantly above all that we ask or think, according to the power that works in us" (Ephesians 3:20). When the Spirit sees us struggling against sin; trying to lift heavy burdens; or fighting the forces of evil all in our own strength, He is deeply grieved, because He knows we can never succeed. He knows however that in His strength we can be "more than conquerors through Him who loved us" (Romans 8:37).

Now, it is possible to be so concerned about losing the Holy Spirit that we may become fearful of even receiving Him. Andrew Murray, the prolific Dutch Reform writer, after stating that God does not retain in us the gift of the Spirit against our will, has this to say: "When Jesus comes by the Spirit to dwell in my heart and live in me, He will actually work out the maintenance of the blessings and regard my whole inner life as His special care. He who believes this truth sees that the life in the blessing of Pentecost, while it can never be relieved of the necessity of watchfulness, is a life that is freed from anxiety and ought to be characterized by continued gladness. The Lord has come into His holy temple. There He will abide and work out everything. He only desires just one thing—that the soul shall know and honor Him as its faithful Shepherd, its almighty keeper. Jesus, who gives the blessing of Pentecost, will certainly maintain it in us." [5]

Water on the Fire

The Holy Spirit can be not only grieved but quenched (1 Thessalonians 5:19). We usually associate "quench" with water. Here Paul uses the word with reference to extinguishing a fire. On the day of Pentecost the Holy Spirit came with fire (Acts 2:4). When the Spirit of prophecy came upon Jeremiah, God put His words in the mouth of the young prophet (Jeremiah 1:4-10). This holy man of God spoke as he was moved by the Holy Spirit (2 Peter 1:21). When later it seemed that he could not continue his prophetic ministry, he said, "His word was in my heart like a burning fire shut up in my bones; I was weary of holding it back, and I could not" (Jeremiah 20:9). Immediately after warning about quenching the Spirit, Paul says, "Do not despise prophecies" (1 Thessalonians 5:20). Obviously there was a rejection of spiritual gifts that Paul was concerned about. Apparently there had been some counterfeits, so people were pouring water over the whole fire of the Holy Spirit. Rather than do this, Paul says, "Test all things; hold fast what is good" (verse 21).

Although my denomination in its early history and in later years was marked by many great movings of the Holy Spirit, there were at least two occasions when the fire of the Holy Spirit was quenched. One such experience took place at Battle Creek College. "Other blessings they desire; but that which God is more willing to give than a father to give good gifts to his children; that Holy Spirit, which is offered abundantly according to the infinite fullness of God, and which, if received, would bring all other blessings in its train—what words shall I use sufficiently to express what has been with reference to it? The heavenly messenger has been repulsed by the determined will. 'Thus far shalt thou go with my students, but no farther. We need no enthusiasm in our school, no excitement. We are much better satisfied to work with the students ourselves.' It is thus that despite has been done to God's gracious messenger, the Holy Spirit." [6] A similar tragedy happened on one other occasion at a large church conference. "Some have treated the Spirit as an unwelcome guest, refusing to receive the rich gift, refusing to acknowledge it, turning away from it, and condemning it as fanaticism." [7] One speaker of authority made the following statement: "Now our meeting is drawing to a close . . . ; there has not been a single break so as to let the Spirit of God in. Now I was saying what was the use of our assembling here together and for our ministering brethren to come in if they are here only to shut out the Spirit of God from the people?" [8]

Rather than quenching the fire of the Holy Spirit, we should be concerned with feeding and filling the fire. Each autumn my wife and I gather and cut hard, dry wood so we can heat our house for the winter using our airtight stove. As the fire dies down we refuel it with oak, fir, or maple, and it burns warm and bright again. We fuel the fire of the Holy Spirit with prayer, Bible study, praise, and Christian fellowship. In fact, sometimes earnest prayer is like throwing gasoline on a fire. There is an explosion of joy and praise that transforms the darkness and coldness into the radiance of God's love.

At a Holy Spirit Fellowship the fire of the Spirit was fueled by wonderful times of prayer, singing, and sharing from God's Word. "A burden I've carried for 40 years has rolled away," one pastor testified with tears of joy that were contagious to all present. Jesus gave the garment of praise in place of the spirit of heaviness; the oil of joy in the place of mourning (Isaiah 61:3). Later a church leader said, "Nothing has transformed my ministry and affected my life like this experience." There will always be those who will try to quench the fire by criticism, false accusations, negative prognostications, doubt, fear, jealousy, and selfishness. I want to praise God right now because the fire is burning in the lives of individuals and in the church, where there is constantly a spirit of total surrender and openness to God.

Unforgivable Blasphemy

Although the Bible speaks of resisting the Spirit (Acts 7:51) and doing despite to or insulting the Spirit of grace (Hebrews 10:29), perhaps the most fearful situation involves blasphemy against the Holy Spirit. This is often referred to as the unpardonable sin. We noticed Jesus' reference to this in Matthew 12:31, 32.

I have spoken to many people who have a deep fear that their sins can never be forgiven. A young lady cried almost uncontrollably, "I know I've committed the unpardonable sin. I know I am lost. I can never be saved." Her adultery had helped break up a beautiful family, and the damage could never be undone. A man who had murdered a store clerk in a robbery attempt wondered if he had committed the unpardonable sin. Like David, he said, "My sin is ever before me" (Psalm 51:3). Is adultery, murder, or breaking one of the other Ten Commandments the sin that can never be forgiven?

John said there is a sin that leads to death and one that does not lead to death (1 John 5:16, 17). He has clearly identified the sin that does not lead to death as the one that is confessed and cleansed from our life (1 John 1:9). It is the work of the Holy Spirit to convict of sin (John 16:8) and give us victory power. So we can conclude that the only sin that leads to death, the only sin that cannot be forgiven, is the one that is not confessed and rejected. D. L. Moody once said, "If a man is troubled about his sins, it is the work of the Spirit; for Satan never yet told him he was a sinner. Satan makes us believe that we are pretty good; that we are good enough without God, safe without Christ, and that we don't need salvation. But when a man wakes up to the fact that he is lost, that he is a sinner, that is the work of the Spirit; and if the Spirit of God had left him, he would not be in that state." [9] A person who turns away from God's love and forgiveness and rejects the Holy Spirit feels no concern or remorse, at least not until the judgment day. If I take the phone off the hook in my hotel room, then the clerk cannot reach me with a wake-up call in the morning and I sleep through contented and happy.

In the context of Matthew 12 the blasphemy against the Holy Spirit seems to relate directly to attributing the work of the Holy Spirit to Satan. When Jesus worked miracles through the Holy Spirit, His enemies said that He was working by the power of Satan. Strangely enough, it was the religious leaders of Jesus' time that committed this sin. In our own time the same situation applies. I have never heard an atheist or critic of Christianity say that Jesus or the Holy Spirit were agents of Satan's power, but I have heard people professing to be Christians pass this judgment on others.

Jackie grew up in a denomination that did not believe in the divinity of Jesus. When the Holy Spirit led her to accept Jesus as her Lord and Saviour and to be baptized in the name of the Father, Son, and Holy Spirit, some of Jackie's former church associates said that she was led by the devil into this evil teaching. After a group of pastors spent a number of days together studying and praying concerning the work of the Holy Spirit, they joyfully shared with their churches some of the miracle-working power of the Spirit and the blessings of a beautiful time of prayer that they had experienced in their meetings. Some critics said that the pastors had been led into emotionalism and false revival by the devil. Is this new?

On the day of Pentecost when the Holy Spirit was poured out, those unmoved by the Holy Spirit said the disciples were drunk. John Wesley, in a letter written to his brother Samuel on May 10, 1739, told of the mighty moving of the Holy Spirit in one of his meetings. Then he records, "A bystander, one John Haydon, was quite enraged by this, and, being unable to deny something supernatural in it, labored beyond all measure to convince all his acquaintance, that it was a delusion of the devil." [10] An early Adventist writer affirms the seriousness of these accusations: "What constitutes the sin against the Holy Ghost? It is willfully attributing to Satan the work of the Holy Spirit." [11]

Does this mean that we will accept every teaching and supernatural event as from God? No, clearly not. In an earlier chapter we noticed some important ways to distinguish truth from error, but sometimes I have learned the hard way not to pass judgment on the basis of preconceived opinions or religious biases.

Some like Diane's friend, Angela, have snubbed the Holy Spirit, bringing grief to His heart of love. Others like Peter's new church associate have quenched the fire of the Spirit in their own lives and are determined to pour water on the flame in any Christian heart. Like Randy, some reject the Spirit, pushing Him away and relying on their own abilities to survive in the world. Jessica was amazed at the judgment expressed by her visitors that she was praying to an untrue God.

Let us keep our hearts open daily and continually to the leading of the Holy Spirit. Ask God to make us aware of the early warning signals of grieving the Spirit in any way. In constant communion with the Spirit we can certainly be safe.

Hurting or Helping the Spirit?

Cohesive Contrasts

The fourth stage of group life after "honeymoon," "disillusionment," and "synthesis" is "culmination." Knowing that your next study together will be the last in this series, plans should be made to begin a new series of studies or to break up as a group. The realization of this can bring a sense of mourning, but also it can bring the anticipation of a new beginning.

Share a memory of your experience in this group that you believe will stay with you the rest of your life.

Consideration of the Word
Study Text: Matthew 12:15-32

What definite interest do you see Satan having in causing us to gradually push the Holy Spirit out of our lives? _____

_____

_____

Stephen accused the Jewish leaders of resisting the Holy Spirit (Acts 7:51). How do you see this happening in Matthew 12:24-30? _____

_____

_____

Review in chapter twelve some reasons that the Holy Spirit can be grieved (Ephesians 4:30) or made "sorrowful." List some things that can make the principle of worldliness dominate our lives. _____

_____

_____

Paul teaches that our bodies are the temple of the Holy Spirit (1 Corinthians 6:19, 20). What are some practical ways I can care for my body and mind so that the temple will be clean and the mind clear? _____

_____

Jesus will not quench the flame or even "smoke" of the Holy Spirit, represented by the flax wick of an oil lamp (Matthew 12:20). Which of the following will quench or which will fuel the fire of the Holy Spirit?

Criticism _____   Personal Bible study _____

Prayer _____   Self-satisfaction _____   Witnessing _____

Cold formalism _____   Small group Bible study _____

Singing praises _____   False accusations _____

Jealousy _____   Spirit-filled worship _____   Other _____

How would you rewrite Matthew 12:31, 32 in your own words? (Here is my version: "Even if you turn against Jesus, there is hope, but if you totally reject the Holy Spirit, there is no hope, because He can no longer lead you to the cross.")

_____

_____

If a person is concerned about sin, he or she has obviously not committed the unpardonable sin. According to John, what sin can always be forgiven (1 John 1:9)? _____

_____

_____

What possible motives can you see for Satan wanting to accuse Jesus and the Holy Spirit of working by His power? _____

_____

_____

_____

The Holy Spirit convicts of sin, righteousness, and judgment (John 16:8). This conviction draws Spirit-filled Christians together in unity. Why is Satan so determined to cause division, dissension, and discord (Matthew 12:25, 30)? __

_____

_____

_____

In Jesus there is no separation. Through the Holy Spirit He gives us power to be more than conquerors (Romans 8:37; Ephesians 3:20). How do you plan to use this power so that the Holy Spirit will not be grieved, quenched, or rejected? .

_____

_____

_____

Conversation With the Lord

First, praise God, remembering that praise is one of your strongest weapons. Praise repels Satan and ministers to God.

Second, pray for specific needs in the group.

Third, pray for needs outside the group. Center especially on anyone you know who appears to be grieving or resisting the Spirit.

Close as usual with the Lord's Prayer.

Committing the Word to Memory

This week, write out Matthew 12:28, 29. Memorize these verses, then share them with someone as soon as possible.

_____

_____

_____

_____

CHAPTER
THIRTEEN
▼

It's Beginning to Rain

I grew up in a beautiful part of New Zealand where rain is fairly common. In fact, the Maoris, when they discovered New Zealand, called the country Aotearoa, "The Land of the Long White Cloud." A few weeks without rain was to us a drought, and most often our "weather prayers" centered on stopping the rain so that some event or ministry would not be washed away. When we moved to Australia, I remember our surprise when my wife and I discovered a whole church congregation praying for rain. Their prayers were earnest and urgent; it had not rained for more than two years, and the situation was desperate.

Have you noticed that the Bible also talks about praying or asking for rain? Hear the words of an ancient prophet: "Ask the Lord for rain in the time of the latter rain" (Zechariah 10:1).

It is quite surprising to discover how much Bible symbolism centers on the agricultural seasons and rains of ancient Palestine. Now, this may not seem very important to us living in our society today, but look at this with me for a moment because it will help us understand some very important factors concerning the Holy Spirit.

Reaping in the Rain

When we plant a garden in Oregon it is always in the spring after the last frost has fallen. We keep our garden watered, and then from late summer into the autumn we reap the harvest. The situation was quite different for the ancient Palestinian people. After the long dry summer the autumn months of October and November brought rain that softened the soil. Now the farmer could harness a couple oxen and plow the ground. In the time of the early or former rain, the seed was sown. These rains continued through the winter, culminating with the spring rains of March or April. This approximated the time of the first month of the Jewish sacred year. These rains of the first month were known as the latter rains, and combined with the warmth of the summer that followed, they matured the crops that were then ready for the harvest.

"Then I will give you the rain for your land in its season, the early rain and the latter rain, that you may gather in your grain, your new wine, and your oil" (Deuteronomy 11:14). When all the grain and fruit harvests were completed, the summer climaxed with joyful celebrations of God's bountiful goodness and wonderful provision for His people.

Unless you are a farmer or gardener, all of this agricultural information may be only of passing interest. That is, until you see a direct connection to your growth with the Lord through the power of the Holy Spirit. For instance, notice how Jesus uses the harvest symbolism: "He answered, 'The one who sowed the good seed is the Son of Man. The field is the world, and the good seed stands for the sons of the kingdom. The weeds are the sons of the evil one, and the enemy who sows them is the devil. The harvest is the end of the age, and the harvesters are angels' "(Matthew 13:37-39, NIV). The King James Version of the Bible says that the harvest is the end of the world. When the book of Revelation gives one of its graphic pictures of the second coming of Jesus, it uses this same symbolism. "And I looked, and behold, a white cloud, and on the cloud sat One like the Son of Man, having on His head a golden crown, and in His hand a sharp sickle. And another angel came out of the temple, crying with a loud voice to Him who sat on the cloud, 'Thrust in Your sickle and reap, for the time has come for You to reap, for the harvest of the earth is ripe' " (Revelation 14:14, 15).

It is in preparation for the harvest that a great final revival, a great outpouring of the Holy Spirit, takes place. This is spoken of by the ancient Hebrew prophets as the latter rain. "Be glad then, you children of Zion, and rejoice in the Lord your God; for He has given you the former rain faithfully, and He will cause the rain to come down for you—the former rain, and the latter rain in the first month. The threshing floor shall be full of wheat, and the vats shall overflow with new wine and oil" (Joel 2:23, 24).

It is exciting to think of the tremendous rain of the Holy Spirit, the latter rain that pours upon the earth before the return of Jesus. I am praying about it—as Zechariah says, asking God for it. I want to be soaked by the latter rain, and I am praying that you will experience it too. Signs indicate that we are living in the beginning of that time of the latter rain right now.

One night I spoke of the Holy Spirit and small group ministries to an earnest crowd of men, women, and young people in a city in the midst of a lush agricultural district in the state of São Paulo, Brazil. About 750 people had driven and walked from the surrounding area, and the meeting ended with a very sincere season of prayer as the Holy Spirit was poured out on us all in a quiet but deeply moving way. Hearts were opened to God in repentance and joy and many decisions were made for a new commitment to Jesus. We had prayed about rain, the latter rain. We had sung "Showers of Blessing," a beautiful hymn based on Ezekiel 34:26: "I will make them and the places all around My hill a blessing; and I will cause showers to come down in their season; there shall be showers of blessing." No sooner had the meeting finished than a tremendous downpour of rain began to fall—not a shower, but a mighty deluge that lasted more than an hour. Somehow that rain symbolized the great outpouring of the Spirit we had prayed about. A few days later in a restaurant owned by a wonderful Spirit-filled Christian lady I met some of the people who had walked home from the meeting that rainy night. "You must have been soaked by the rain," I said, thinking about how wet I got just running to the car. One of the ladies replied through Daniel dos Santos, my inspirational and Spirit-filled translator, "To have been present at a meeting like we had with such beautiful prayer and evidence of the Holy Spirit was worth it all. I walked home rejoicing in the rain."

Today, as the song says, it's beginning to rain. Billy Graham in his concluding address at a great evangelism conference emphasized his belief in the falling of the rain. "I believe that as we approach the latter days of the coming of the Lord it could be a time also of great revival. We cannot forget the possibility and promise of revival, the refreshing of the latter days (the 'latter rain' of Hosea), or the outpouring of the Spirit promised in Joel 2:28 and repeated in Acts 2:17. That will happen right before the advent of the Lord Jesus Christ. James seems to associate the latter rains with the return of Christ. Evil will grow worse, but God will be mightily at work at the same time. I am praying that we will see in the next month and year the 'latter rains'; a rain of blessings, showers falling from heaven on all of the continents before the coming of the Lord." [1]

Historically in the Christian church the outpouring of the Holy Spirit on the disciples in Jerusalem on the day of Pentecost has been called the former or early rain. The great revival moving corporately and collectively among born-again Christians around the world just before the return of Jesus has been called, as we have noticed, the latter rain.

Before we look at some very interesting factors about the prophetic, corporate latter rain, I want to notice with you three other partial fulfillments of the early and latter rain that have helped me a great deal in understanding the final mighty work of the Holy Spirit.

Jesus and the Disciples in the Rain

Have you noticed the early and latter rain experiences in the life and ministry of Jesus? Jesus was created in Mary by the Holy Spirit (Luke 1:35). Later Luke records that "the Child grew and became strong in spirit, filled with wisdom; and the grace of God was upon Him" (Luke 2:40). Jesus had not only the strength of the Spirit, but the spiritual gift of wisdom (1 Corinthians 12:8). The grace of God was upon Him, which, as we have noticed, indicates the power of the Holy Spirit that filled Jesus from birth.

Jesus' three and a half years of latter rain began at His baptism. "God anointed Jesus of Nazareth with the Holy Spirit and with power, who went about doing good and healing all who were oppressed by the devil, for God was with Him" (Acts 10:38). In Jesus' ministry there was complete evidence that He did not receive the Spirit in a limited measure (John 3:34; Luke 4:18). And it was through this indwelling Spirit that Jesus was able to perfectly reveal the Father to all who sincerely acknowledged Him (John 14:9).

Because of the mighty working of the Holy Spirit in the life of Jesus, three groups that were vowed enemies of each other, the Pharisees, Sadducees, and Romans, joined together to destroy the Saviour. On the day of resurrection, to the complete confusion of His enemies, Jesus was made alive in the Spirit (1 Peter 3:18). Finally, it was the Holy Spirit who signaled to humanity on earth that Jesus had been restored to His position of authority and ministry in heaven (Acts 2:33).

I was really amazed to discover that what happened to Jesus was a microcosm of what would happen to His church. The interrelationship between the New Testament events and Christian history is incredible. Look at this again in the context of Jesus' disciples. Although the outpouring of the Holy Spirit at Pentecost was evidently the early rain for the Christian church, it is not hard to see that the disciples had their latter rain experience with the events of Pentecost and all that followed. But did they have an early rain experience? It appears that this happened on the very day of the resurrection. "And when He had said this, He breathed on them, and said to them, 'Receive the Holy Spirit' " (John 20:22). The fruitage of this is clearly seen in the pre-Pentecostal joy of the disciples.

"And they worshiped Him, and returned to Jerusalem with great joy, and were continually in the temple praising and blessing God" (Luke 24:52, 53). They prayed continually in the Spirit and by the Spirit were led into a unity defying division (Acts 1:14; 2:1).

We are very familiar with the disciples' "latter rain" experience on the day of Pentecost. The Spirit came like a mighty rushing wind. There were tongues of fire; the disciples received miraculous spiritual gifts including tongues and healing. And in biblical support for what had happened they quoted the latter rain passage from Joel 2 (Acts 2:1-21). The ministry of the disciples was completely dominated, as was Jesus' ministry, by the power of the Holy Spirit. Anglican canon Michael Green, in his classic *Evangelism in the Early Church,* says, "Paul uses an interesting word for this assurance in preaching, 'plerophoria,' which appears to suggest that the preachers were so full of the Spirit of God, so persuaded of the truth and relevance of their message, that it overflowed from them and men received what they had to say, 'Not only in word, but also in power and in the Holy Spirit and with full conviction.' " [2] This absolute Spirit-inspired conviction enabled the disciples to turn the world of their time upside down (Acts 17:6).

It was not only preaching and teaching in public and house churches that changed the world. There was more. Just as Jesus revealed the character of the Father, so these disciples had begun to reflect the character of Jesus. "Now when they saw the boldness of Peter and John, and perceived that they were uneducated and untrained men, they marveled. And they realized that they had been with Jesus" (Acts 4:13). Michael Green also writes of the miracle of this transformation. "If the loving fellowship of the Christian community was one prerequisite for effective evangelism, another was a transformed character. The New Testament records lay great emphasis on this. The transformation of John, that son of thunder, into the apostle of love, or of Peter, that mercurial hothead, into a man of Rock, is an essential part of the logic of the gospel. This is what contact with Christ does for a man. He becomes changed into likeness to Christ from one degree of glory to another by the Lord, the Spirit." [3]

You will notice that another parallel with Jesus' experience just jumps out at us from Scripture and history. The disciples were opposed violently by two groups who really had no love for each other. Both Jewish leaders and Roman authorities tried to overthrow Christianity. Most of the disciples died martyrs' deaths, as did many of the early

Christians, but nothing could stop the onward movement of Spirit-filled Christianity. In fact, it reached, Paul said, into all the world and to every creature in his day (Colossians 1:6, 23).

Modern Christians in the Rain

As the early and latter rain experience was evident in the life of Jesus and the disciples, so it can be a reality for every true Christian today. You can experience it right now, and I pray that you are. As we studied in an earlier chapter, it is at conversion that a person becomes in a special sense the dwelling place of the Holy Spirit (Ephesians 1:13, 14; Romans 8:9). In this way like the dry ground after the long Palestinian summer the early rain brings vitality and growth in the gifts and graces in the Spirit. "For I will pour water on him who is thirsty, and floods on the dry ground; I will pour My Spirit on your descendants, and My blessing on your offspring; they will spring up among the grass like willows by the watercourses" (Isaiah 44:3, 4).

Paul explained to Titus how the prophecy in Isaiah 44 is fulfilled as you and I accept Jesus as our Saviour. "Not by works of righteousness which we have done, but according to His mercy He saved us, through the washing of regeneration and renewing of the Holy Spirit, whom He poured out upon us abundantly through Jesus Christ our Savior" (Titus 3:5, 6). Our reception of the Holy Spirit at conversion is confirmed externally by our water baptism when we are buried in the name of the Father, Son, and Holy Spirit (Matthew 28:19, 20) and we rise to walk in a new life of spiritual power (Romans 6:3, 4).

This new life that we experience is like the springing up of the seed in the Palestinian soil. Believe it or not, we are "created to be like God in true righteousness and holiness" (Ephesians 4:24, NIV). This is incredible! Look at it carefully, and you will see why I am amazed. Just as Jesus revealed the character of God and the disciples astonished their enemies by revealing the character of Jesus, so we also are re-created to reflect the holiness and righteousness of our Lord. Humanly speaking, this is impossible, and no true Christian ever feels worthy of such honor, but by the power of the Holy Spirit true holiness is the destiny of all who surrender daily to Jesus. If someone recognized this holiness in you, I am sure you would be surprised and, like Paul, say, "By the grace of God I am what I am" (1 Corinthians 15:10).

At every stage of the true Christian life there is a deeper repentance, an ever-increasing hatred of sin. Allergies are more than a nuisance. Some people are afflicted with allergies to dust, pollen, gluten, or oranges. The body does not appreciate these substances, and there is a strong urge to keep clear of them. So through the Holy Spirit we develop an allergy to sin.

Unless the early rain work of the Holy Spirit takes place in our lives, there can be no readiness for the latter rain. Occasionally in Palestine there would be a terrible autumn season with no rain softening the ground or germinating the seed. Then the latter rains could not do more than wash the hard ground in spring. The only fruitage was famine and tragedy for the hungry people.

The daily baptism or filling of the Christian life by the Holy Spirit can be likened to a personal latter rain. Although this, of course, does not fulfill the prophetic significance of the final outpouring of the Holy Spirit, individually you can be completely filled with the Spirit every day. Do not wait for some later time to be filled with the Spirit. You can have a personal latter rain experience right now. "We may have had a measure of the Spirit of God, but by prayer and faith we are continually to seek more of the Spirit. It will never do to cease our efforts. If we do not progress, if we do not place ourselves in an attitude to receive both the former and the latter rain, we shall lose our souls, and the responsibility will lie at our own door. 'Ask ye of the Lord rain in the time of the latter rain.' Do not rest satisfied that in the ordinary course of the season, rain will fall. Ask for it. . . . The convocations of the church, as in camp meetings, the assemblies of the home church, and all occasions where there is personal labor for souls are God's appointed opportunities for giving the early and the latter rain." [4] This writer also goes on to say, "We must pray that God will unseal the fountain of the water of life. Let us, with contrite hearts, pray most earnestly that now, in the time of the latter rain, the showers of grace may fall upon us. At every meeting we attend our prayers should ascend, that at this very time God will impart warmth and moisture to our souls." [5]

Is our reception of the baptism of the Holy Spirit dependent upon all others around us receiving it? Jesus all alone was filled with the Holy Spirit daily, as were the disciples after Pentecost who, apart from their own small group were, like Jesus, surrounded by open hostility. John on the island of Patmos was filled with the Holy Spirit even though the majority of churches he addressed needed to repent (Revelation 2; 3). John Wesley's Spirit-filled ministry closed the doors of his denomination to him, forcing him to preach in the fields and begin the small groups and societies that led to Methodism.

It is important not to apply the conditions for the final, prophetic, corporate outpouring of the latter rain of the Holy Spirit to the individual reception of the filling of the Holy Spirit. For instance, must the whole church be in perfect unity before I can receive the filling of the Holy Spirit? No. Unity in the church can be achieved only as individuals are filled with the Spirit. Paul calls this the unity of the Spirit (Ephesians 4:3). The fruit of the Spirit is love which is the basis of unity. I noticed this statement in an old Christian magazine. "We are to seek most earnestly to be of one mind, of one purpose. The baptism of the Holy Spirit, and nothing less, can bring us to this place." [6]

Exactly the same situation applies as far as sin is concerned. God pours out His Spirit on imperfect, although not deliberately disobedient, people. It is this that gives the strength and victory power over sin. Peter calls this the "sanctification of the Spirit" and says that it is possible to obey the truth through the Spirit (1 Peter 1:2, 22). When I was 18 I liked the way this was explained in *The Desire of Ages,* and I still like it today. "He who is trying to reach heaven by his own works in keeping the law is attempting an impossibility. There is no safety for one who has merely a legal religion, a form of godliness. The Christian's life is not a modification or improvement of the old, but a transformation of nature. There is a death to self and sin, and a new life altogether. This change can be brought about only by the effectual working of the Holy Spirit." [7] "The Spirit was to be given as a regenerating agent, and without this the sacrifice of Christ would have been of no avail. . . . Sin could be resisted and overcome only through the mighty agency of the third person of the Godhead, who would come with no modified energy, but in the fulness of divine power." [8] If you are not claiming the victory power of the Holy Spirit, you are shortchanging yourself today. You can live in victory. You do not have to be defeated.

Now, a thought may enter our minds that causes some concern. Jesus and the disciples were opposed by determined enemies, so will Spirit-filled Christians today have to face the same opposition? Unfortunately, as we have noticed in our chapter on spiritual warfare, attacks will come from the remains of our sinful nature within us and the evil forces outside us, but as Paul says, we will triumph in Jesus (2 Corinthians 2:14).

Rejoicing in the Latter Rain

Now for the last lap before history's checkered flag. James couples rain terminology to the second coming of Jesus. "Therefore be patient, brethren, until the coming of the Lord. See how the farmer waits for the precious fruit of the earth, waiting patiently for it until it receives the early and latter rain. You also be patient. Establish your hearts, for the coming of the Lord is at hand" (James 5:7, 8). James said to wait patiently, but I seem to be impatient for the latter rain to fall. The time of the latter rain will be the most exciting period of earth's history. The Holy Spirit will move in people's lives with a power never before seen. One reason for this is that finally there are people on earth who are so totally surrendered to God that they would rather die than knowingly sin. Through the grace of God they reflect the beauty of Jesus' character. Satan also works with intense anger to discourage and destroy, but God's true people are gathered together from all denominations and religions. With joyful expectation, claiming only the righteousness of Jesus, they wait eagerly to be "reaped" at the great final harvest.

Are you wondering how this incredible climax takes place? Just study with me now a few verses of Scripture, and we will see everything fitting perfectly together.

We have noticed that Joel applied the latter rain terminology to the events preceding the reaping of the harvest (Joel 2:22-24). This is explained as the great outpouring of the Holy Spirit before the end of the world (verses 28-32). It is now that the faithful remnant will be delivered (verse 32). This remnant represents the people who call on the name of the Lord. Their total faith and trust is in God, and they are "harvested" at the second coming of Jesus. Jesus summarized all of this in His great second coming discourse by picturing the final spreading of the gospel around the world: "And this gospel of the kingdom will be preached in all the world as a witness to all the nations, and then the end will come" (Matthew 24:14).

Just as Jesus Himself and the disciples at the time of the historic early rain were surrounded with counterfeits of the Holy Spirit and attacks of Satan, so Jesus warns of this again. "Then many false prophets will rise up and deceive many. And because lawlessness will abound, the love of many will grow cold. But he who endures to the end shall be saved" (Matthew 24:11-13). Enduring to the end will be possible and even enjoyable through the power of the Holy Spirit. That is why Jesus told the story of the ten virgins. Although they all went through a period of spiritual slumber, in the end the five wise women were ready for the wedding because their supply of oil was sufficient to keep their lamps burning to the end. (Notice how the symbolism of oil was used for the Holy Spirit in such places as Zechariah 4:1-7; 1 Samuel 16:13.)

It is very interesting to discover how the prophecy of the latter rain of the Holy Spirit in Joel and the final preaching of the gospel in Matthew 24 is explained in Revelation 14. Just before the harvest God's Spirit-filled people will bring about the final fulfillment of the preaching of the messages of the three angels. The remnant that Joel talks about are identified as those who "keep the commandments of God and the faith of Jesus" (Revelation 14:12). If you are not familiar with the vivid symbolism of Revelation, you may want to join a small group using the *Window to Revelation* Bible study guides. [9]

The last book of the Bible is a great revelation of Jesus and is inspired by the Holy Spirit. The central emphasis of Revelation is that through the blood of Jesus and the power of the Holy Spirit, you can be an overcomer and have victory in every crisis of life. When the checkered flag falls, you can be in front of all the tendencies to evil within you or attacks of evil from around you. Revelation reveals God's "remnant" as winners in the end.

Bible scholars have seen the latter rain pictured also in the symbolism of the angel in Revelation 18:1: "After these things I saw another angel coming down from heaven, having great authority, and the earth was illuminated with his glory." Warning is given in Revelation 18 of the downfall of the deceptive forces of evil. God's people are called out of confusion represented by Babylon, and the rejoicing of the harvest and second coming of Jesus is seen in Revelation 19.

If Revelation is a mystery to you at this time, do not get bogged down trying to work out all the complex imagery that is there. Just remember that the final latter rain of the Holy Spirit will be the last great spiritual revival that will separate the whole world into two groups. As Jesus said, there will be just one true group of His Spirit-filled people. "And other sheep I have which are not of this fold; them also I must bring, and they will hear My voice; and they will be one flock and one shepherd" (John 10:16). As with the early disciples, great grace will be upon these true people of God in the time of the latter rain. In fact, only through grace are they at all prepared for earth's final harvest. "As the members of the body of Christ approach the period of their last conflict, 'the time of Jacob's trouble,' they will grow up into Christ, and will partake largely of His

Spirit." [10] "But near the close of earth's harvest, a special bestowal of spiritual grace is promised to prepare the church for the coming of the Son of man." [11]

The last great revival will be opposed by two extremes who have no love for each other, but unite in their opposition of God's remnant people. One extreme has been deceived by false revival. Their religion consists of emotionalism, noise, and excitement, and rejects as legalism the claims of God's Word for holy living according to the commandments of God and the faith of Jesus. They reject the true revival because they link it to legalism (see 2 Thessalonians 2:9, 10).

On the other hand, some are cold and legalistic, revealing a spirit of judgmentalism and accusation. They work to draw as many as possible away from the true revival and the true church of God (see Acts 20:30). These people reject the true revival because they link it to the liberalism of the false revival.

To the liberal and legalistic religious enemies will be linked a civil power as happened in the experience of Jesus. The legalistic Pharisees and the liberal Sadducees linked with the secular power of Rome to destroy Jesus. So it will be in the last days. Revelation pictures the scene in which there will be death decrees and various boycotts against those who are filled with the Spirit in the final latter rain revival (Revelation 13).

Young and old who are filled with the Holy Spirit continue to seek rain in the time of the latter rain. God's prophecy concerning His spiritual remnant will soon be fulfilled. "For He will finish the work and cut it short in righteousness, because the Lord will make a short work upon the earth" (Romans 9:28). Conversions will come so quickly that even the church will be surprised. Many children of Christian families that have drifted away from fellowship with God's people will return. Prominent national leaders will, like Nicodemus, publicly take their stand on the side of truth.

What a day! It is beginning now. "It's beginning to rain." Rain in western Oregon rarely makes the headlines. Sometimes it has been known to rain continually for a month. But one day in Cairo, Egypt, I noticed that the front page headlines in the newspaper boldly and triumphantly exclaimed, "First Rain for Three Years." I was there when those few sprinkles of rain fell, and on a dry land they were impressive. But in a place where rain is common, it is possible to put up an umbrella and not even notice what is happening. Today as we approach the time of the latter rain we must not put up our spiritual umbrellas so that the rain will be falling on hearts all around us and we will miss out on the blessing. It's beginning to rain. Let's walk, run, and rejoice in the beautiful rain of the Holy Spirit.

It's Beginning to Rain

Cohesive Contrasts

As you come to your last group meeting studying these guides on the subject of the Holy Spirit, you may want to take some time to evaluate ways in which the group has met or exceeded your initial expecations. You should also be ready to move into a new series of study guides or to discontinue meeting as a group. Here is a positive affirmation question to begin this group time together.

If you could give one gift or present to each group member, what would it be?

Consideration of the Word
Study Text: Joel 2:23-32

The prophet Joel seemed to be very familiar with agricultural terminology. What impression do you get from his use of such words as "glad" and "rejoice" as you compare Joel 2:23, 24 with verse 32? _____

_____

_____

What would you list as some reasons for Christians to be earnestly praying for the "rain" in this time of the latter rain just before the return of Jesus?_____

_____

Although Jesus was filled with the Holy Spirit from birth, what effects do you see Jesus' "latter rain" experience having on His ministry (Acts 10:38)? _____

_____

_____

Historically it seems that the outpouring of the Holy Spirit at Pentecost was the church's "early rain" experience. What significance do you see in Peter's use of Joel's "latter rain" passage (Acts 2:16-21)?

Peter was confused _____ The prophecy applied to both events _____ Pentecost was the "coming of the great and dreadful day of the Lord" _____ Pentecost was the disciples' "latter rain" experience _____ Other _____

Paul says that the Holy Spirit creates us to be like God in true righteousness and holiness (Ephesians 4:24). How does the thought of your personal "latter rain" holiness make you feel?

Excited _____ Amused _____ Doubtful _____

Very humble _____ Confused _____ Proud _____

Grateful _____ Other _____

Joel likens the "remnant" who are saved to the harvest at the end of the world. How does the Holy Spirit use the preaching of the gospel to gather together the final remnant (Matthew 24:14; Revelation 14:6-16)? _____

_____

_____

From your study of this chapter, list some similarities you see between the attacks that came on Jesus and the early Christians and the opposition against the final latter rain revival. _____

The latter rain of the Holy Spirit may be poured out on people all around us and we do not even see it or recognize it. What would you consider the most important precautions a person can take against this tragedy? _____

_____

_____

_____

Have you seen or read of any signs that the "rain" is beginning to fall? Why not share these with your group? _____

_____

_____

We are excited about the latter rain and rejoice in every shower, yet James says we must wait patiently (James 5:7, 8). What encouragement can you share with your group members who are impatient for the harvest? _____

_____

_____

_____

Conversation With the Lord

First, "pray for rain in the time of the latter rain." Pray for deepening repentance and true holiness in Jesus.

Second, claim God's victory power for each person in the group. Pray for specific needs.

Third, pray for God's leading in beginning a new group.

By now the Lord's Prayer with its seven specific sections, should be a very important part of your group and Christian experience. Conclude your group again today by praying this prayer together.

Committing the Word to Memory

This week, write out Joel 2:23, 24. Memorize these verses, then share them with someone as soon as possible.

_____

_____

_____

_____

Bible References to the Holy Spirit

Genesis 1:2—The Spirit hovered over the waters.
   6:3—My Spirit will not always strive with man.
   41:38—Joseph—a man in whom the Spirit of the Lord is.

Exodus 31:3—Bezaleel—filled with the Spirit of God in wisdom, in understanding, in knowledge, and in all manner of workmanship.

Numbers 11:25, 26, 29—The Spirit of God on Moses was shared with 70 elders; when they received it they prophesied.
   24:2—The Spirit of God came upon Balaam, and he prophesied.
   27:18—Joshua, a man in whom is the Spirit.

Judges 3:10—Spirit of the Lord came upon Othniel, younger brother of Caleb.
   6:34—Upon Gideon.
   11:29—Upon Jephthah.
   13:25—Upon Samson from birth.
   14:6—Upon Samson for strength.
   14:19—Upon Samson.
   15:14—Upon Samson.

1 Samuel 10:6—By the Spirit you will be turned into another man.
   10:10—Upon Saul, who prophesied.
   11:6—Upon Saul.
   16:13—Upon David.
   16:14—Departed from Saul.
   19:20—Upon messengers of Saul, who prophesied.
   19:23, 24—Upon Saul, who prophesied, and lay naked.

2 Samuel 23:2—Spirit of the Lord spoke by David.

1 Kings 18:12—Obadiah was afraid the Spirit would carry Elijah away.

2 Kings 2:9—Double portion of the Spirit on Elisha.
2:16—The Spirit took Elijah up.

2 Chronicles 15:1—Upon Azariah, for prophecy.
20:14—Upon Jahaziel, for prophecy.
24:20—Upon Zechariah.

Job 33:4—The Spirit of God has made me.

Psalm 51:11—Do not cast me away from Your presence, and do not take
Your Holy Spirit from me.
104:30—You send forth Your Spirit; they are created.
106:33—Israel rebelled against the Spirit.
139:7—Where can I go from Your Spirit?

Proverbs 1:23—I will pour out My Spirit on you.

Isaiah 63:10—They rebelled and grieved His Holy Spirit.
63:11—Put His Holy Spirit within them (Israel).
63:14—The Spirit caused the beast to rest.

Ezekiel 2:2—The Spirit entered Ezekiel when God spoke.
3:12—The Spirit lifted Ezekiel up.
3:14—The Spirit lifted him up and took him away.
3:24—The Spirit entered, and spoke words to Ezekiel.
8:3—The Spirit took Ezekiel in vision to Jerusalem.
11:1—The Spirit took Ezekiel again.
11:5—The Spirit fell upon Ezekiel and said, "Speak!"
11:19—A new spirit can be gotten.
11:24—The Spirit took Ezekiel to Chaldea.
18:31—A new heart and a new spirit.
36:26—A new heart and new spirit are from Holy Spirit.
37:1—The Spirit took Ezekiel to valley of dry bones.
37:14—The Spirit makes dry bones live.
39:29—The Spirit makes us to know God.
43:5—The Spirit carried away Ezekiel to God's temple.

Daniel 4:8, 9, 18; 5:11, 14—They knew Daniel was full of the Spirit of God.

Joel 2:28—The Spirit brings dreams and visions in last days.

Micah 2:7—The Spirit of the Lord is not restricted.
  3:8—Micah knew he was full of power by the Spirit.

Haggai 2:5—The Spirit was with Zerubbabel, but he needed assurance.

Zechariah 4:6—Not by might or power, but by the Spirit.
  7:12—The Spirit came by former prophets.
  12:10—He will pour out the Spirit of grace and supplication, and we will look on Him whom we have pierced.

Matthew 1:18—Mary was with Child of the Holy Spirit.
  1:20—The Child was conceived of the Holy Spirit.
  3:11—He will baptize you with the Holy Spirit and fire.
  3:16—They saw the Spirit descend like a dove.
  4:1—Jesus was led by the Spirit into the wilderness.
  10:20—The Spirit will speak in us in our hour of trial.
  12:18—The Spirit was given to Jesus to declare justice.
  12:28—Demons cast out by the Spirit of God.
  12:31—Blasphemy against the Spirit will not be forgiven men.
  12:32—Whoever speaks against the Holy Spirit, it will not be forgiven.
  22:43—David in the Spirit spoke concerning Jesus.
  28:19—Baptize them in the name of the Father and of the Son and of the Holy Spirit.

Mark 1:8—He will baptize you with the Holy Spirit.
  1:10—The Spirit descended like a dove.
  3:29—He who blasphemes against the Holy Spirit never has forgiveness.
  12:36—David spoke by the Holy Spirit.
  13:11—When you are arrested, the Holy Spirit will give you what to speak.

Luke 1:15—John the Baptist was filled with the Holy Spirit, even from the womb.

1:35—The Holy Spirit will come upon Mary, and the power of the Highest will overshadow.

1:41—Elizabeth was filled with the Holy Spirit.

1:67—Zacharias was filled with the Holy Spirit and prophesied.

1:80—Jesus grew and was strong in the Spirit.

2:26—The Holy Spirit revealed to Simeon that he would see the Messiah.

2:27—Simeon came by the Spirit into the Temple.

3:16—He will baptize you with the Holy Spirit and fire.

3:22—Holy Spirit descended in bodily form like a dove.

4:1—Jesus was filled with the Holy Spirit and led by the Spirit.

4:14—Jesus returned to Galilee in the power of the Spirit.

4:18—The Spirit of the Lord is upon Me.

11:13—The Holy Spirit given to them that ask Him.

12:10—To him who blasphemes against the Holy Spirit, it will not be forgiven.

12:11, 12—When you are arrested, the Holy Spirit will teach you in that very hour.

John 1:32—The Spirit descended like a dove.

1:33—Jesus—it is He who baptizes with the Holy Spirit.

3:5—Unless born of water and the Spirit, we will not see the kingdom.

3:6—That which is born of the Spirit is spirit.

3:8—Born of the Spirit is like the wind—it comes and goes as it wishes, and you don't know where.

3:34—God does not give the Spirit by measure.

4:23—True worshipers worship in Spirit and truth.

4:24—God is Spirit.

6:63—The Spirit gives life. Words of Jesus are spirit and life.

7:38, 39—He who believes in Me, out of his heart will flow rivers of living water. This He spoke concerning the Spirit, whom those believing in Him would receive; for the Holy Spirit was not yet given, because Jesus was not yet glorified.

11:33—Jesus groaned in the Spirit.

14:16, 17—The Spirit is the Helper. The Spirit of truth, whom the world cannot receive because it neither sees Him nor knows Him, dwelt with disciples before Pentecost.

14:26—The Helper, the Holy Spirit, whom the Father will send in My name, will teach you all things, and bring to your remembrance all things that I said to you.

15:26—The Spirit of truth proceeds from the Father; He will testify of Jesus.

16:7-11—The Spirit convicts of sin, judgment, and righteousness.

16:13, 14—The Spirit of truth will guide you into all truth, what He hears He speaks, He will tell of things to come, and glorify Jesus.

20:22—Jesus breathed on them and said, "Receive the Holy Spirit."

Acts 1:2—Jesus gave commandments through the Holy Spirit.

1:5—John baptized with water, but you shall be baptized with the Holy Spirit.

1:8—You shall receive power when the Holy Spirit has come upon you.

1:16—David spoke by the Holy Spirit.

2:4—They were filled with the Holy Spirit and spoke with tongues.

2:17, 18—Pentecost fulfilled Joel's promise of the Spirit.

2:33—Jesus received the promise of the Holy Spirit and poured it out on His disciples.

2:38—Repent and be baptized and you shall receive the gift of the Holy Spirit.

4:8—Peter was filled and spoke by the Holy Spirit.

4:31—They prayed, the place was shaken, they were filled with the Holy Spirit, they spoke with boldness.

5:3, 4—Ananias lied to the Holy Spirit, God.

5:9—Ananias and Sapphira tempted/tested the Spirit.

5:32—The Holy Spirit is a witness given to those who obey God.

6:3—Seek out men full of the Holy Spirit.

7:51—The Pharisees always resisted the Holy Spirit.

7:55—Stephen was full of the Holy Spirit and saw the glory of God.

8:15—The apostles prayed for others, that they might receive the Holy Spirit. For as yet He had fallen upon none of them. They had only been baptized in the name of the Lord Jesus. Then they laid hands on them, and they received the Holy Spirit.

8:29—The Spirit spoke words to Philip.

8:39—The Spirit caught Philip away.

9:17—Ananias laid hands on Paul that he might receive the Holy Spirit.

9:31—The churches had the comfort of the Holy Spirit.

10:19—The Spirit spoke words to Peter.

10:38—God anointed Jesus with the Holy Spirit.

10:44—While Peter was speaking, the Holy Spirit fell upon all those who heard the Word.

10:45-48—Gentiles received the Holy Spirit before they were baptized, and spoke with tongues.

11:12—The Spirit told Peter to go with the Gentiles.

11:15, 16—As Peter spoke, they were filled with the Holy Spirit.

11:24—Barnabas was full of the Holy Spirit.

11:28—Agabus in the Spirit warns of a great worldwide famine.

13:2—As they ministered to the Lord and fasted, the Holy Spirit said to separate Paul and Barnabas.

13:4—Paul and Barnabas were sent out by the Holy Spirit.

13:9—Paul, filled with the Holy Spirit, preached.

13:52—The disciples were filled with joy and the Holy Spirit.

15:8—God acknowledged them by giving them the Holy Spirit just as He did to us.

15:28—It seemed good to the Holy Spirit not to put more heavy burdens on the Gentiles.

16:6, 7—The Holy Spirit forbade them to go to Asia or Bithynia.

18:5—Paul was constrained by the Spirit to testify to Jews.

19:2-6—People who were baptized by John had not received the Holy Spirit, but had repented. They were baptized in the name of the Lord, and Paul laid hands on them and they received the Holy Spirit and spoke with tongues and prophesied.

20:23—The Holy Spirit testified in every city to Paul, saying that chains and trouble awaited him.

20:28—The Holy Spirit appoints overseers to shepherd.

21:4—Certain disciples through the Spirit warn Paul about going to Jerusalem.

21:11—The Holy Spirit prophesied through a man to Paul.

28:25—The Holy Spirit spoke through Isaiah.

Romans 1:4—The Spirit of holiness.

5:5—The love of God is poured out in our hearts by the Holy Spirit who was given to us.

7:6—We serve in newness of the Spirit.

8:1—No condemnation to those who walk according to the Spirit.

8:2—Law of the Spirit makes free from law of sin and death.

8:4—Righteous requirement of law fulfilled in those who walk according to the Spirit.

8:5—Those who live according to the Spirit set their minds on the things of the Spirit.

8:9—In the Spirit, if the Spirit dwells in you. If you have not the Spirit, you don't belong to Christ.

8:10—If Christ is in you, the body is dead, but the Spirit is life because of righteousness.

8:11—If the Spirit dwells in you, He will also give life to mortal bodies through the Spirit.

8:13—By the Spirit we put to death the deeds of the body.

8:14—Those led by the Spirit are sons of God.

8:15—The Spirit of adoption cries out, "Abba, Father."

8:16—The Spirit bears witness with our spirit that we are children of God.

8:23—Even we, who have the firstfruits of the Spirit, groan for complete adoption, or redemption of our body.

8:26—The Spirit helps in our weaknesses in prayer.

8:27—The Spirit makes intercession for saints according to the will of God.

9:1—My conscience bearing witness in the Holy Spirit.

14:17—The kingdom of God is righteousness, peace, and joy in the Holy Spirit.

15:13—Abound in hope by the power of the Holy Spirit.

15:16—The offering of the Gentiles sanctified by the Holy Spirit.

15:19—Mighty signs and wonders by the power of the Spirit.

15:30—Paul speaks in the love of the Spirit.

1 Corinthians 2:4—Paul's preaching was in demonstration of the Spirit and of power.

2:10—God revealed secret things through the Spirit; the Spirit searches deep things of God.

2:11—Only the Spirit knows the things of God.

2:12—When we receive the Spirit, we know the things of God.

2:13—Speak with words that the Holy Spirit teaches.

2:14—Things of the Spirit are foolishness to natural man.

3:16—Body is temple of God; the Spirit dwells in you.
6:11—We are washed, sanctified, justified by the Spirit.
6:19—Body is temple of the Holy Spirit.
7:40—Paul thinks he has the Spirit of God on celibacy.
12:3—Only by the Spirit can we confess Jesus as Lord.
12:4—It is the same Spirit but different gifts.
12:7—Gifts are manifestations of the Spirit for the profit of all.
12:8-10—Gifts are by the same Spirit.
12:11—The Spirit works the gifts and gives as He wills.
12:13—By one Spirit we were all baptized.

2 Corinthians 1:22—He has sealed us and given us the Spirit as a deposit.
3:3—Deeds are done by the Spirit.
3:6—The Spirit gives life.
3:8—Ministry of the Spirit more glorious than the law, which caused light on Moses' face.
3:17—The Lord is the Spirit. Where the Spirit is, there is liberty.
3:18—We are transformed by the Spirit into the image of the Lord.
5:4, 5—The Spirit is the guarantee that our mortality will be swallowed up by eternal life.
6:4-6—Commend ourselves as ministers of God by the Holy Spirit.
13:14—The communion of the Holy Spirit be with you all.

Galatians 3:2—The Spirit received by hearing of faith.
3:3—The Spirit, not flesh, makes perfect.
3:5—The Spirit and His miracles supplied by the Lord by the hearing of faith.
3:14—Receive the promise of the Spirit through faith in the redemption of Christ.
4:6—Sons receive the Spirit of His Son, crying out, Abba, Father!
4:29—Children of flesh persecute children of the Spirit.
5:5—Through the Spirit we eagerly wait for the hope of righteousness of faith.
5:16—Walk in the Spirit, and we will not fulfill lust of flesh.
5:17—The Spirit and flesh are contrary to one another, so that we do not do what we wish.
5:18—But if we are led by the Spirit, we are not under the law.
5:22, 23—Fruit of the Spirit.
5:25—If we live in the Spirit, let us walk in the Spirit.

6:8—He who sows to the Spirit will of the spirit reap everlasting life.

Ephesians 1:13—Heard the word, trusted, in whom you, having believed, were sealed with the Holy Spirit.
    2:18—Through Jesus we have access to the Father by the Spirit.
    2:22—We are being built by the Spirit into habitation for the Father.
    3:5—The Spirit reveals knowledge not known before.
    3:16, 17—The Spirit strengthens with might the inner man, that Christ may dwell in our hearts through faith; being rooted and grounded in love.
    4:3—The unity of the Spirit.
    4:4—One body and one Spirit.
    4:30—Do not grieve the Holy Spirit of God, by whom you were sealed for the day of redemption.
    5:9—Fruit of the Spirit is in goodness, righteousness, and truth.
    5:18, 19—Be filled with the Spirit, singing psalms, hymn, and spiritual songs.
    6:17—Sword of the Spirit is the word of God.
    6:18—Prayer and supplication in the Spirit.

Philippians 1:19—Salvation through prayer and supply of the Spirit.
    2:1—Fellowship of the Spirit.

Colossians 1:8—Love in the Spirit.

1 Thessalonians 1:5—The gospel came in power and the Holy Spirit.
    1:6—Received the word with joy of the Holy Spirit.
    4:8—Sexual immorality rejects God, who has given us His Holy Spirit.

2 Thessalonians 2:13—Salvation through sanctification by the Spirit and belief in the truth.

1 Timothy 3:16—God was justified in the Spirit.
    4:1—The Spirit prophesies about loss of faith in the end.
    4:14—Gift given to Timothy through laying on of hands.

2 Timothy 1:14—Keep the good things committed to you by the Holy Spirit.

Titus 3:5—He saved us through the washing of regeneration and renewing of the Holy Spirit.

Hebrews 2:4—God bearing witness with signs, wonders, miracles, and gifts of the Holy Spirit.
   3:7—The Holy Spirit says, "Today."
   6:4—Impossible to renew those who were once enlightened and have become partakers of the Holy Spirit.
   9:8—The Holy Spirit indicating the way into the Holiest of All was not yet made manifest while the first tabernacle was still standing.
   10:15—The Holy Spirit also witnesses.
   10:29—The Spirit can be insulted to our destruction.

1 Peter 1:2—Sanctification of the Spirit.
   1:11—Prophets of old had the Spirit.
   1:12—The gospel preached by the Holy Spirit.
   1:22—Purify souls through obeying the truth through the Spirit.
   3:18—Christ was made alive by the Spirit.
   4:6—Live according to God in the Spirit.
   4:14—If you are reproached for the name of Christ, then the Spirit of Christ rests on you.

2 Peter 1:21—Prophecy came by the Holy Spirit.

1 John 3:24—We know God abides in us by the Spirit He has given.
   4:2—You know the Spirit of God if He confesses that Jesus came in the flesh.
   5:6—The Spirit bears witness of Jesus' sacrifice, because the Spirit is truth.

Jude 19—Sensual persons who cause divisions have not the Spirit.
   20—Praying in the Holy Spirit.

Revelation 1:10—John was in the Spirit on the Lord's Day.
   2:7, 11, 17—The Spirit says to the churches.
   2:29; 3:6, 13, 22—The Spirit says to the churches.
   4:2—John in the Spirit immediately.
   11:11—The Spirit of God entered the two witnesses.
   14:13—The Spirit speaks that the saints may rest.

17:3—The Spirit carried John away to wilderness.
21:10—The Spirit carried John away to New Jerusalem.
22:17—The Spirit and the bride say, "Come [Lord Jesus]!"

References

Chapter One

[1] Ellen G. White, *Testimonies for the Church* (Mountain View, Calif.: Pacific Press Pub. Assn., 1948), vol. 1, p. 383.
[2] _____, *The Acts of the Apostles* (Mountain View, Calif.: Pacific Press Pub. Assn., 1911), p. 50.

Chapter Two

[1] Ellen G. White, *The Desire of Ages* (Mountain View, Calif.: Pacific Press Pub. Assn., 1940), p. 305.
[2] _____, *Gospel Workers* (Washington, D.C.: Review and Herald Pub. Assn., 1948), p. 286.
[3] _____, *Steps to Christ* (Washington, D.C.: Review and Herald Pub. Assn., 1956), p. 52.

Chapter Three

[1] White, *The Acts of the Apostles*, p. 49.
[2] Andrew Murray, *The Believer's Full Blessing of Pentecost* (Minneapolis: Bethany House Pub., 1984), p. 22.

Chapter Four

[1] Dwight L. Moody, *Secret Power* (Ventura, Calif.: Regal Books, 1987), pp. 29, 30.
[2] White, *The Desire of Ages*, p. 672.
[3] *Ibid.*
[4] _____, *Evangelism* (Washington, D.C.: Review and Herald Pub. Assn., 1946), p. 616.
[5] _____, *The Desire of Ages,* p. 669.
[6] Samuel Chadwick, *The Way to Pentecost* (Berne, Ind.: Light and Hope Pub., 1937), pp. 47, 48.
[7] White, *Testimonies*, vol. 5, p. 512.

Chapter Five

[1] J. H. Waggoner, *The Spirit of God* (Battle Creek, Mich.: SDA Pub. Assn., 1877), pp. 35, 36.
[2] White, *Testimonies*, vol. 1, pp. 158, 159.
[3] _____, *My Life Today* (Washington, D.C.: Review and Herald Pub. Assn., 1952), p. 58.
[4] _____, *Life Sketches* (Mountain View, Calif.: Pacific Press Pub. Assn., 1915), pp. 36-38.
[5] _____, *Christ's Object Lessons* (Washington, D.C.: Review and Herald Pub. Assn., 1941), pp. 147, 148.

Chapter Six

[1] W. W. Prescott, *The Promise of the Holy Spirit* (Payson, Ariz.: L.O.A. Books, 1989), pp. 9f.

[2] White, *The Desire of Ages*, p. 672.

[3] Kevin Wilfley, *Studies on the Holy Spirit* (Portland, Oreg.: Oregon Conference of SDAs, 1989), p. 21.

[4] Ben Carson, *Gifted Hands* (Washington, D.C.: Review and Herald Pub. Assn., 1990), pp. 57-59.

[5] In G. B. Thompson, *The Ministry of the Spirit* (Washington, D.C.: Review and Herald Pub. Assn., 1914), p. 117.

[6] White, *The Desire of Ages*, p. 436.

[7] *Ibid.*, p. 181.

[8] *Ibid.*, p. 250.

[9] Don and Ruthie Jacobsen, *Window to John's Gospel* (College Place, Wash.: Color Press, 1990). For information on these 21 study guides on the Gospel of John, call 509-525-6030.

Chapter Seven

[1] White, *Testimonies*, vol. 3, p. 377.

[2] _____ , *Steps to Christ,* pp. 51, 52.

[3] Arthur L. White, *Ellen G. White: The Progressive Years* (Washington, D.C.: Review and Herald Pub. Assn., 1986), pp. 428, 429.

[4] E. G. White, *Evangelism*, p. 616.

[5] _____ , *Testimonies,* vol. 1, p. 158.

[6] *Ibid.*, p. 163.

[7] _____ , *Early Writings* (Washington, D.C.: Review and Herald Pub. Assn., 1945), p. 72.

[8] Wilfley, *Studies on the Holy Spirit*, pp. 72, 73.

[9] George Canty, *The Hallmarks of Pentecost* (London: Marshall Pickering, 1989), p. xv.

[10] Ellen G. White, *Selected Messages* (Washington, D.C.: Review and Herald Pub. Assn., 1958), book 2, pp. 35, 36.

[11] *Ibid.*, p. 57.

Chapter Eight

[1] E. G. White, *The Acts of the Apostles*, p. 45.

[2] R. A. Torrey, *The Person and Work of the Holy Spirit* (Grand Rapids: Academie Books, 1974), p. 106.

[3] Roy C. Naden, *Your Spiritual Gifts* (Berrien Springs, Mich.: Ipd., 1989). A manual, inventory, videos, and small group study guides are available.

[4] William McRae, *The Dynamics of Spiritual Gifts* (Grand Rapids: Zondervan Pub. House, 1967), pp. 19, 20.

Chapter Nine

[1] C. Peter Wagner, *Your Spiritual Gifts* (Glendale, Calif.: Regal Books, 1979), p. 237.

[2] See *Adventist Review,* July 23, 1989.
[3] Ellen G. White, *The Great Controversy* (Mountain View, Calif.: Pacific Press Pub. Assn., 1950), p. 612.
[4] _____ , *Testimonies,* vol. 9, p. 126.

Chapter Ten

[1] Wagner, *Your Spiritual Gifts*, p. 101.
[2] In *Christianity Today*, Aug. 20, 1990, p. 19.
[3] E. G. White, *Christ's Object Lessons*, p. 300.

Chapter Eleven

[1] E. G. White, *Steps to Christ*, p. 58.
[2] E. J. Waggoner, *The Glad Tidings* (Mountain View, Calif.: Pacific Press Pub. Assn., 1978), p. 112.
[3] Christopher Wordsworth, *New Testament* (London: Rivingtons, 1870), vol. 2, p. 68.

Chapter Twelve

[1] Albert Barnes, *Notes on the New Testament* (London: Blackie and Son), vol. 7, p. 93.
[2] James A. Stewart, *Heaven's Throne Gift* (Fort Washington, Pa.: Christian Literature Crusade, 1971), pp. 146, 147.
[3] Ellen G. White, *Counsels on Diet and Foods* (Washington, D.C.: Review and Herald Pub. Assn., 1938), pp. 55, 56.
[4] _____ , *The Ministry of Healing* (Mountain View, Calif.: Pacific Press Pub. Assn., 1942), p. 127.
[5] Murray, *The Believer's Full Blessing of Pentecost*, p. 64.
[6] Ellen G. White, *Fundamentals of Christian Education* (Nashville: Southern Pub. Assn., 1923), p. 434.
[7] _____ , *Testimonies to Ministers* (Mountain View, Calif.: Pacific Press Pub. Assn., 1962), p. 64.
[8] _____ , in A. V. Olson, *Thirteen Crisis Years* (Washington, D.C.: Review and Herald Pub. Assn., 1981), p. 300.
[9] Moody, *Secret Power*, p. 122.
[10] John White, *When the Spirit Comes With Power* (Downers Grove, Ill.: InterVarsity Press, 1988), p. 78.
[11] E. G. White, *Testimonies*, vol. 5, p. 634.

Chapter Thirteen

[1] J. D. Douglas, ed., *Let the Earth Hear His Voice* (Minneapolis: World Wide Publications, 1975), p. 1446.
[2] Michael Green, *Evangelism in the Early Church* (London: Hodder and Stoughton, 1970), p. 118.
[3] *Ibid.*, p. 183.

[4] E. G. White, *Testimonies to Ministers*, p. 508.

[5] *Ibid.*, p. 509.

[6] _____ , in *Review and Herald,* June 10, 1902.

[7] _____ , *The Desire of Ages,* p. 172.

[8] *Ibid.*, p. 671.

[9] Garrie F. Williams, *Window to Revelation* (College Place, Wash.: Color Press, 1990).
For further information on these 20 study guides, call 509-525-6030.

[10] E. G. White, *Testimonies*, vol. 1, p. 353.

[11] _____ , *The Acts of the Apostles,* p. 55.

For additional reading
on the Holy Spirit

Coming of the Comforter. LeRoy Froom's definitive study on the promise, coming, filling, and symbols of the Holy Spirit answers some of our most vital questions regarding the Spirit and shows how we can experience the power and joy He longs to bring us. Paper, 320 pages. US$7.95, Cdn$9.95.

Books that equip you
to share God's love

Christ's Way of Reaching People. Dr. Philip Samaan takes a close look at the way Christ related to others and shows how we can apply these principles to witnessing today. Paper, 160 pages. US$9.95, Cdn$12.45.

Small Group Outreach. Kurt Johnson's step-by-step guide to successful small group Bible study tells you everything you need to know to organize a group and lead its members toward a new life in Christ. Paper, 95 pages. US$6.95, Cdn$8.70.

Add more joy and meaning
to your prayer life!

ABCs of Bible Prayer. Based on a simple formula—ask, believe, and claim—Glenn Coon's popular book is filled with wonderful stories of answered prayer. Paper, 208 pages. US$7.95, Cdn$9.95.

Incredible Answers to Prayer. Roger Morneau is a man of incredible faith. When he prays, things happen. And it's exciting! He shares these exhilarating experiences of answered prayer with you in this gripping book. Paper, 96 pages. US$6.95, Cdn$8.70.

Practical Pointers to Personal Prayer. Using her own deeply personal and triumphant experience, Carrol Johnson Shewmake guides you step by step toward satisfying communion with your heavenly Father. She tells how she lost the boredom and guilt that had choked her lifeline to God and found intimate two-way conversation in its place. Paper, 128 pages. US$7.95, Cdn$9.95.

Ask your bookseller or order from ABC Mailing Service, P.O. Box 1119, Hagerstown, MD 21741. Send check or money order. Enclose applicable sales tax and 15 percent (minimum US$2.50) for postage and handling. Prices and availability subject to change without notice.